PEEPSHOW

PEEPSHOW

MEDIA AND POLITICS IN AN AGE OF SCANDAL

LARRY J. SABATO

MARK STENCEL

S. ROBERT LICHTER

ROWMAN & LITTLEFIELD PUBLISHERS, INC.
Lanham • Boulder • New York • Oxford

ROWMAN & LITTLEFIELD PUBLISHERS, INC.

Published in the United States of America
by Rowman & Littlefield Publishers, Inc.
4720 Boston Way, Lanham, Maryland 20706
http://www.rowmanlittlefield.com

12 Hid's Copse Road
Cumnor Hill, Oxford OX2 9JJ, England

British Library Cataloguing in Publication Information Available

Library of Congress Cataloging-in-Publication Data

Sabato, Larry.
    Peepshow : media and politics in an age of scandal / Larry J. Sabato,
Mark Stencel, S. Robert Lichter.
       p.   cm.
    Includes bibliographical references and index.
    ISBN 0-7425-0010-1 (cloth : alk. paper)
    1. Press and politics—United States.   2. United States—Politics and
government—1993–   3. Government and the press—United States.
I. Stencel, Mark.   II. Lichter, S. Robert.   III. Title.

PN4888.P6 S236 2000
070.4'49324'0973—dc21   99–088697

Printed in the United States of America

♾™ The paper used in this publication meets the minimum requirements
of American National Standard for Information Sciences—Permanence of
Paper for Printed Library Materials, ANSI/NISO Z39.48–1992.

As a disseminator of the news, the paper shall observe the decencies that are obligatory upon a private gentleman.

What it prints shall be fit reading for the young as well as for the old.

—Two of Eugene Meyer's "principles" for the Washington Post, *which were published after he purchased the newspaper in 1933. The complete principles are still posted in the newspaper's lobby and are reaffirmed in its style manual for reporters and editors.*

Contents

Acknowledgments

A project of this sort, involving so many details and so little time, is really a collaboration with many individuals whose names deserve our recognition.

At Rowman & Littlefield, executive editor Jennifer Knerr has been our most encouraging and patient advocate, as has publisher Jonathan Sisk. You may never heard of this little book if not for the marketing ideas of Nancy Rothschild, and it would not have been worth your time if not for the project editing of Dorothy Bradley. Generous research support from the Markle Foundation also paved our way to publication.

As our primary researcher, journalist Suzette McLoone proved herself to be an excellent digger, cajoler, negotiator, and sounding board. She was crucial to the careful assembly and navigation of this unwieldy dirigible. Matthew Wikswo at the University of Virginia's Center for Governmental Studies played an equally major role in guiding our project to a safe landing, managing the complexities of the editorial and promotional process. Along the way we had significant help from Mary Carroll Gunning and the rest of the staff at the Center for Media and Public Affairs in Washington, the politics staff of washingtonpost.com, and from Alex Theodoridis and others at the Center for Governmental Studies in Charlottesville, including our diligent student researchers, Ade Patton and Brett Farrell.

The editing of this project was made easier by three professionals whose involuntary servitude to this endeavor we will never adequately acknowledge: Lisa Todorovich, Sandra Stencel, and especially Christine Sneed Stencel, each of whom has shown time and again that love, friendship, and tough editing are not incompatible. Christine's many personal sacrifices for this project exceed those of the authors.

In interviews and less formal discussions, several friends and colleagues offered us their time, insights, leads, good ideas, and inspiration. Among them: Peter Baker, Dan Balz, Ken Bode, Dennis Britton, David Broder, Fred Brown, Tim Burger, Kathleen deLaski, Len Downie, Juliet Eilperin, Doug Feaver, Dan Froomkin, Susan Glasser, Natalie Green, Bill Hamilton, Walter Isaacson, Bob Kaiser, Marvin Kalb, Morton Kondracke, Eric MacDicken, Ann McDaniel, Paul Rodriguez, Harrison Ullmann, and John Yang. The prompt and patient transcriptions of our friend Caroline Schor MacDicken helped us sort through it all efficiently. The assistance of our source Bob from Wirthington is also greatly appreciated.

Our conclusions are our own, as are any errors in the text, for which the authors take sole responsibility.

Prologue

The Scene of the Crime

The line political reporters draw between private and public life is perhaps more blurry than ever before. With increasing regularity, that blurry line is the smudged chalk outline of an ambitious politician.

For both politicians and journalists, deciding when private matters are the public's business is almost always challenging. Competition from new and alternative news sources makes those decisions even more complicated. Mainstream news outlets—newspapers, magazines, broadcast and cable television—no longer serve as almost exclusive gatekeepers of information about those who hold or seek elected office. At the same time, evolving public standards and increasing competitive pressures for a shrinking news audience are changing the ways editors and producers determine when and how to delve into the private lives of political figures. These forces make some editorial decisions seem almost arbitrary.

- House Speaker–designate Bob Livingston resigns from Congress, admitting that he on occasion "strayed" from his marriage, after learning that his sex life is under investigation by pornographic magazine publisher Larry Flynt. At the same time, mainstream media outlets ignore long-standing but unconfirmed rumors of an extramarital affair that involves retiring Speaker Newt Gingrich and a House committee aide twenty-three years his junior. Instead of reporting the story, traditional news organizations wait for a supermarket tabloid to break the news—seven months after Gingrich leaves office.

- The same supermarket tabloid uses DNA analysis from the independent counsel probe of President Bill Clinton to conduct a paternity test on the teenage son of a one-time Arkansas prostitute. Although most news organizations ignore this story, millions of Americans learn about the paternity test from Jay Leno's monologues on NBC's *Tonight Show*. The test ultimately clears Clinton.

- Newspapers across the country run wire stories and commentary on sixteen-year-old Sarah Gore after police catch the vice president's daughter holding an open beer can in a car outside a high school party in suburban Washington. A year later, editors decide not to run stories about why Sarah's little brother, Albert III, transferred from one prestigious private school to another. A Washington magazine subsequently reports that the move followed an incident in which the first school disciplined the seventh grader for an alleged marijuana offense—a detail that is confirmed but surprisingly never published by other news organizations.

The press attention focused on the thirteen-month investigation and impeachment of President Clinton has put the press on trial for both its excesses and its oversights. To some, the coverage of President Clinton's sexual relationship with a former low-level White House functionary was an alarming invasion of privacy, a political smear. To others, it was a criminal matter that prompted a long-overdue examination of a pattern of reckless behavior that endangered the moral and ethical standing of the presidency. At the state and local level, candidates now regularly answer probing media questions about adultery, substance abuse and other private behavior—queries that even presidential candidates once weren't expected to answer. Nonetheless, many stories about politicians' private lives still never make it into print or on the air, even after news about those with similar pasts and public responsibilities is reported.

Just what are the rules for politicians and journalists in the aftermath of Washington's biggest sex scandal? When are a public official's or candidate's private affairs fair game and when are they out of bounds? The public, the press and those they cover are divided.

Are extramarital relationships newsworthy? Two married Republicans, New York City mayor Rudolph W. Giuliani and South Carolina governor David Beasley, had different answers during their campaigns for second terms, when both officials denied unconfirmed and largely unsubstantiated allegations that they had had affairs with their female communications directors. Giuliani, who was reelected in 1997, said in a CNN interview that a politician's performance in office should be more important to voters than his or her performance in private. "I think the prying that goes on into private lives doesn't really add very much to decisions that you make about people," Giuliani said. "What's going on in their private life, in their marriage? I think actually we have gone way too far in that regard." Beasley, on the other hand, told local reporters during his losing 1998 campaign that he would have considered his personal behavior newsworthy—if the rumors about him were true. "If I fail in that standard, I want you to knock my teeth out," Beasley said. "I want you to rip me up and down this state. I want you to embarrass me, humiliate me and destroy me because I will have done wrong."[1]

Different media organizations, not to mention different types of media organizations, have their own, sometimes contradictory, answers to the same question about fidelity. In Beasley's case, the *Point*, an alternative monthly newspaper in the state capital, first addressed the unproven rumors about the governor's alleged affair in a 1996 gossip item that was widely read in state political circles. The publication, which reported the allegations in its "Loose Lips" column, justified publishing the story because of Beasley's conservative Christian positions on family matters: "This column firmly upholds the notion that people's private lives are their own business. But when people make a business out of telling other people how to live their private lives, they make their own foibles fair game." The *Columbia State* newspaper took a more conservative approach to the same story, extensively investigating and then largely ignoring the gossip, even as the unsubstantiated story swept the capital.

Two years later, during another wave of rumor, *State* editor Mark Lett discussed the issue directly with Beasley's campaign. "Their position was it was not true," Lett told the *Washington Post* later. "Our position was that we can't prove it to be true, so there it sat." A national news report about the rumor in *Time* magazine, however, brought a strong denial from the governor, whose public statements were covered by news media across South Carolina. The *State* and other news organizations disclosed that previous reporting did not substantiate the rumors, but that detail was often lost in much of the subsequent coverage of Beasley's response and its expected political fallout.[2]

The fidelity of elected officials and other personal matters are of little concern to most Americans, despite the attention such stories sometimes get in the news. Beasley, for instance, lost his reelection race, but debates over the Confederate flag and legalized gambling were far more significant issues in his defeat than rumors about his fidelity. The same is true in national politics. In December 1998, during the debate over the impeachment of President Clinton and amid a series of revelations about past relationships involving several members of Congress, almost 80 percent of respondents said in a *Washington Post*–ABC News national survey that they disapproved of the attention paid to questions about extramarital affairs. In a poll conducted three months later, after the Senate acquitted Clinton, 75 percent of respondents to a poll by the Pew Research Center for the People and the Press said news organizations were "driving controversies" rather than "reporting the news" by covering the personal and ethical behavior of public figures.[3]

The Pew Center's polling also suggests that a candidate's personal life is not a major campaign issue for most Americans, even in presidential politics. In a September 1999 survey, strong majorities thought the press should almost always report stories about a presidential candidate's spousal abuse (71 percent), income tax evasion (65 percent), exaggerated military record (61 percent) and exaggerated academic record (61 percent). But there was significantly less interest in reports about a candidate's ongoing affairs (43 percent), sexuality (38 percent), past drinking (36 percent) or cocaine use (35 percent). Less than a quarter of those surveyed (23 percent) said the press should almost always report on a past affair or marijuana use. Less than a third said the press should routinely delve into other personal issues—psychiatric treatment, antidepressant use, even abortions.[4]

Editorial judgment is not always, if ever, a perfect reflection of public opinion. News organizations have a journalistic obligation to try to inform all readers and viewers, even the sizable minority to whom a candidate's or elected official's personal morality is a decisive voting issue. In the Pew Center poll, for example, a significantly higher percentage of Republicans than Democrats said the press should cover many of the personal issues mentioned above, with the division as high as 27 percent on stories about ongoing affairs.[5]

Scandal coverage also can have positive effects on the political process. Intense scrutiny by the press and political opponents can drive away scalawags, increase public accountability and foster realistic attitudes about the human fallibility of elected leaders. But the costs of today's politics-by-scandal outweigh any remedial effects. While public trust in politicians is near all-time lows, confidence in the media is no higher, and participants on both sides say the emphasis on scandal is reducing voter turnout, distracting from important policy debates and discouraging the best politicians and best journalists.

Many forces drive this destructive process. One significant factor has been the intense scrutiny of President Clinton, whose lies about his sexual relationship with former White House intern and staffer Monica S. Lewinsky were the subject of Clinton's impeachment. The Senate acquitted the president in February 1999, although a federal judge in Arkansas later held Clinton in contempt of court and fined him for his false testimony about Lewinsky in a dismissed sexual harassment case filed by a former Arkansas state employee, Paula Jones. The Lewinsky probe and the Jones civil lawsuit both became forums for airing numerous charges of infidelity and sexual misconduct, many of which were based on information that likely would not have met the standards of most news organizations without a legal hook. More significantly, these charges set the tone for a continuous media "feeding frenzy" that dominated the political process for most of Clinton's second term in office, with numerous public officials, candidates and their family members facing intense personal scrutiny. New technology, intense competition, alternative media sources, and cutthroat campaign tactics propelled journalists in a painful quest for information on long-secret affairs, unproven rumors and minor indiscretions. Pious political pronouncements—often about morality and the president's behavior—served as invitations for scrutiny, promising possible leads to stories of galling hypocrisy.

Editors and producers are quick to point out that they do not share common "rules" that dictate how and where to play news stories, relying instead on personal "news judgment." But news decision-makers generally do consider three key factors when deciding whether to delve into private behavior of public figures:

- Facts: Does the evidence substantiate the behavior, or is there merely rumor? What do those involved, directly and indirectly, say?
- Context: When did the behavior occur? Does it have any relationship to a person's public duties, responsibilities or statements? What were the source and timing of the information?
- Interest: Will readers or viewers care? How important is the information?

These general considerations are of limited value. Like economists, journalists rarely operate in a perfect theoretical vacuum that allows editors to offer precise equations that explain their decisions. Facts are murky and often disputed. Statements contradict. Sources have motives, and news consumers are fickle. These considerations make news decisions seem erratic and confusing to those outside media circles. And those decisions are rarely explained by those who make them, mostly because an explanation would reveal subjective choices made by people who prefer to think of themselves as passive observers rather than active participants in the stories they present.

This volume examines the editorial decisions behind news stories involving the private lives of more than two dozen political figures, mostly in the 1996 and 1998 election cycles and the early stages of the 2000 campaign for president. (See exhibit A for brief summaries of the primary case studies.) Our focus is on the decisions that editors and producers make to either run with or "spike" certain stories. Chapter 1 details our proposed guidelines for investigating the private lives of politicians and the standards by which we evaluate our case studies. Chapter 2 describes the forces that drive such coverage, and chapter 3 points a finger at journalists' unindicted coconspirators in political scandal coverage—the politicians themselves. Chapter 4 describes some of the worst journalistic practices our case studies reveal, while chapter 5 explains some of the consequences. Chapter 6 offers some hope that political reporting may not be as bad as it often seems—as well as recommendations on ways to raise editorial standards, increase journalistic credibility, and provide reasonable privacy protections to those who seek public office.

In his August 17, 1998, televised speech admitting his relationship with Monica Lewinsky, President Clinton said there were some questions no American should have to answer. "Even presidents have private lives," Clinton said.[6] Their opinions about Clinton's deeds notwithstanding, most Americans agree and would extend that protection to others in political life. But the reluctance of traditional news organizations to clearly define that "zone of privacy" creates a default rule, set by late-night comedians, grocery store tabloids, crusading pornographers and other media voices. That rule: Anything goes.

1

Precedent

The press is on trial with readers and viewers. The charge: Unnecessary violation of the privacy of politicians and their families. Mainstream American political journalism offers an indicting array of examples in recent years, including coverage of extramarital affairs, office romances, divorces, drug use, drinking, sexuality, illegitimate children and plain, unsubstantiated rumor. Individual cases can be made to justify almost any news story that fell into these categories. Collectively, however, the predominance of such so-called character questions is eroding the credibility of political journalists and turning American democracy into a sort of peepshow or soap opera. Public opinion surveys suggest that journalists have stepped over the line most—but not all—Americans would set for legitimate editorial inquiry. Whether reporters, editors and producers are in fact guilty of violating the standards of their own profession depends on whether there really are any standards in an age of multimedia competition among information sources.

Journalists do not like to follow the rules, largely because they do not like to set them—especially when it comes to politicians. "It is hard to have guidelines, since stories keep coming along that defy previous precedents," said Walter Isaacson, managing editor of *Time* magazine. "However I tend to be cautious about delving into a candidate's private life and it tends to make me uncomfortable. There's a smell test: You can usually tell whether you're considering a story because it is truly relevant to a candidate's character or, on the other hand, because it's titillating and you're just trying to be sensational."[1]

For Leonard Downie Jr., executive editor of the *Washington Post*, there are no blanket rules, although there are broad standards that cover politicians' private lives—with wide latitude for individual news judgment. "We take everything on a case-by-case basis depending on the two standards we impose. First, can it be proven to be true? And second, is it relevant to the candidacy?"[2]

But who draws the line between relevant and irrelevant? Morton Kondracke, editor of the Capitol Hill newspaper *Roll Call* and a regular television commentator, applies a Potter Stewart test to this question, paraphrasing the Supreme Court justice's famous definition of obscenity: "I don't know what the line is, but I know it when I see it."[3]

While the public shows consistently little interest in the private lives of elected officials, that view is not unanimous, with greater interest in a candidate's personal foibles among Republicans than Democrats, according to survey data.[4] The need to serve the news interests of all readers might argue then for complete examination of each and every candidate's closet. But since some stories about the personal lives of political figures—such as news about their children—rarely, if ever, appear in print or on the air, the effective news standard is clearly less than full disclosure.

Once, editors required a clear intersection between a politician's private behavior and his public responsibilities to deem a story newsworthy. But many stories fall in a broad zone between private and public. Does any candidate who has ever posed for a family photo for a campaign brochure make his or her marriage or parenting an issue? Does voting on abortion issues make an abortion in one's own past an issue? While these are subjective decisions for individual journalists and news organizations, a candidate's public response to any such question in effect legitimizes a subject for coverage elsewhere.

Judging the behavior of the press requires more specific guidelines for gauging the relevancy of particular stories. In more than a decade of research, analysis and journalism, the authors have endorsed a "fairness doctrine" that offers rough editorial suggestions for separating personal matters that generally should—and should not—be considered relevant and newsworthy. Our proposed guidelines and accompanying qualifiers, first presented in Larry J. Sabato's *Feeding Frenzy* in 1991, provide a useful prism through which to begin an examination of the political case studies discussed in detail throughout this chapter and the rest of this volume.[5]

None of the conduct described below automatically disqualifies a politician from holding public office. Such decisions are for the voters, who will always have to choose their leaders from a pool of flawed human beings. Our suggestions merely offer a tool to journalists. It is up to individual editors, reporters and producers to decide how best to inform their readers and viewers, each of whom may have a unique standard of conduct for the political leaders he or she entrusts.

Our proposal simply divides private conduct into two categories: behavior that generally should be covered by the press and behavior that in most cases should not. Some of the examples cited below and throughout this book violate our own standards for news reporting but are essential to understanding the decisions that political editors and senior producers now routinely face.

PRIVATE LIFE SUBJECT TO PUBLICATION AND BROADCAST

1. All of a candidate's personal and professional finances (investments, transactions, earnings, taxes, and so on), and the

3

financial arrangements of his or her spouse or immediate family to the extent that they directly bear on the financial well-being of the candidate.

Media reports about rumors of drug use, heavy drinking and alleged draft-dodging by Texas governor George W. Bush during the early stages of the 2000 presidential campaign were controversial. But news reports about Bush's business dealings in Texas before he became governor, even allegations with little substantiation, drew few objections from the public or from media critics. Among the financial matters that journalists investigated: a 1990 offshore oil-drilling contract with Bahrain, which the Persian Gulf emirate awarded to a company that Bush advised as a board member during his father's White House administration, and Bush's $15 million share of the 1998 sale of the Texas Rangers baseball team, in which he had invested a little over $600,000.[6] The public and the press are far more comfortable rummaging through a candidate's checkbook than his or her bedsheets and liquor cabinet.

The same comfort level with a candidate's finances was evident in coverage of President Clinton, whose much-investigated Whitewater real-estate investment and related matters were treated far less gingerly by reporters during his first term in office than Paula Jones's allegations about his sexual misconduct.[7] One reason for the difference between those cases is that money often suggests opportunities for corruption that directly relates to official responsibility. Another reason is that financial transactions by their very nature are often simpler to document than allegations of extramarital sex or substance abuse. Government and private audits, financial disclosure statements and bank transactions are more easily obtained than lipstick-smeared collars and semen-stained dresses.

In financial matters, however, there is an element of interpretation that often means the case is never closed in the eyes of the press. Republican Bob Dole's 1996 campaign for president answered many questions about his family's financial dealings that his aides had already addressed during his 1988 campaign for the White House. Among them: Elizabeth Dole's purchase of a Florida condo from agriculture executive Dwayne Andreas, whose company benefited from her husband's actions in Congress, and the Doles' knowledge of business dealings involving a former Dole fund-raiser who administered a blind trust for Elizabeth Dole and profited by some of the fund's activities. Had Elizabeth Dole remained a candidate in the race for the 2000 presidential nomination, those questions undoubtedly would have resurfaced.[8]

2. *A candidate's health to the extent that it may affect his or her performance in office.*

The case of Texas Democrat Henry B. Gonzalez, who represented his San Antonio congressional district from 1961 to 1999, will not surprise anyone who is cynical about the importance of those who serve in government. The former House Banking Committee chairman spent more than half of his final two-year term in Congress at home in Texas recovering from a heart ailment. The Texas media took little notice of the congressman's extended absence until a July 1998 story in the *Houston Chronicle*—almost a year after Gonzalez's last vote in the House. But even then few were willing to comment on the record about the legendary lawmaker's decision to stay in office rather than retire before the end of the term, as he originally promised. Gonzalez returned to work two months later—fourteen months after he'd left and shortly before his son won the campaign to succeed him.[9]

Generally speaking, medical problems are not as much of an issue in congressional races as they are in presidential campaigns. Some members of Congress have held office and even been reelected despite debilitating illnesses. Republican Karl Mundt of South Dakota, for instance, suffered a severe stroke in 1969 but served out the remaining three years of his final term without ever returning to the Capitol. More recently, voters in Texas Democrat Frank M. Tejeda's district reelected him with more than 70 percent of the vote while he underwent treatment for a malignant brain tumor. Tejeda died in January 1997, days after taking the oath of office for his third term at a private hospital ceremony in San Antonio. If Tejeda had not represented a safe Democratic district, his health might have been a factor in his last campaign, as it was in the 1992 North Carolina Senate race, in which voters ousted incumbent Terry Sanford a month after heart surgery sidelined the seventy-five-year-old Democrat.[10]

Medical matters are a more significant issue in presidential politics. Voters care about the health and stamina of the person they will entrust with the nation's most demanding job, as well as oversight of the U.S. nuclear arsenal. Candidate Paul E. Tsongas, a Democratic runner-up in the 1992 White House race, often bristled when asked about the cancer that drove him from the Senate after his first and only term ended in 1984. But in August 1992, the same month Tsongas would have accepted his party's presidential nomination had he bested Clinton in the primaries, doctors found a growth in the former senator's abdomen. A biopsy performed two weeks after the November 1992 election determined that the growth was cancerous and Tsongas began chemotherapy treatment the following month. A president-elect facing such a serious medical problem in the period between Election Day and his or her inauguration might cause a serious political crisis.

Despite Tsongas's irritation with questions about his cancer, the scrutiny of his health during the 1992 primaries was completely justified—especially since political ambition is itself an incurable disease. "The last living cell that will die in my body is the desire to be president of the United States," Tsongas once told reporters. "And there is no treatment for it."[11]

3. *Any incident or charge that reaches the police blotters or a civil or criminal court.*

For those who make laws, any violation, no matter how minor, is a legitimate news story—and often a political death sentence. A car accident in 1995 cost North Carolina Republican David Funderburk a $25 fine, $60 in court expenses, and ultimately a second term in the House of Representatives. Even after he pleaded no contest to a minor traffic offense, the former Eagle Scout and his wife insisted she was driving when their car forced a van off a remote stretch of highway. Witnesses at the scene said that the congressman was in fact behind the wheel and switched places with his wife after driving a half-mile down the road from the accident, which injured two adults and their four-year-old daughter. Funderburk also bruised his reputation in the accident, which the local press covered extensively. A year later, Funderburk's Democratic rival used the incident in a damning television ad in a successful campaign to oust the GOP freshman.[12]

Some routine police matters involving political figures, from fender-benders to marital spats, inevitably draw more media attention than they deserve. In June 1999, Representative James Moran's wife called police to the couple's home in Alexandria, Virginia, to break up an argument. No charges were filed against the Virginia Democrat, who once made national headlines after he and another lawmaker got into a shoving match just off the House floor. But Mary Moran, who filed for divorce the day after the incident in the Moran home, told police and local reporters that her husband grabbed and pushed her. In his own court filing a month after the altercation, the congressman said his wife "routinely threatened to humiliate and embarrass the defendant, and to destroy his career by making false and scurrilous accusations against him to the police and the press." In this case, the *Washington Times* and the *Washington Post* both played stories about the local congressman's domestic policy squabble appropriately inside the newspaper.[13] While fertile ground for gossip, the information in court and police files is often unfair and unbalanced—notoriously so in divorce cases. While newsworthy, such stories require careful handling.

4. *Sexual activity where there is a clear intersection between an official's public and private roles; for example, relationships with staff members and lobbyists, where elements of coercion or conflict of interest inherently exist.*

President Clinton is far from the only politician to have been caught in a compromising position with a member of his staff. Republican Mike Bowers was perhaps his party's best hope for winning the Georgia governorship since Reconstruction, before he admitted to a longstanding extramarital relationship with his secretary in 1997. Bowers's strong support with Christian conservatives suffered after his confession, and the former frontrunner suddenly faced GOP primary challengers, falling poll numbers and calls from prominent Republicans that he drop out of the race. Bowers's standing took another hit the following April, when former secretary Anne Davis began granting interviews about their affair to *George* magazine and local media. Davis said Bowers provided ongoing financial support of $400 to $600 a month throughout their fifteen-year relationship. Bowers immediately ended the payments, which he said his wife supported as "humanitarian" help for Davis to deal with a heart condition. But a financial and romantic relationship of this sort with a paid state employee raised thorny questions that reporters and some previously supportive state party leaders could not ignore. Ultimately those questions dogged the candidate throughout the primary campaign and cost him his party's nomination—although Bowers's stronger than expected showing in the primary almost pushed the Republican race into a runoff.[14]

Relationships like the Bowers–Davis affair are not uncommon in politics or in any professional setting, including newsrooms, colleges and other institutions. Unfortunately, justified scrutiny of such affairs should not give way to unfair—and usually unsubstantiated—speculation about other close relationships between political figures and key advisers of the opposite sex. Cristyne F. Lategano, the communications director for New York City mayor Rudolph Giuliani, attributed rumors and media reports about her relationship with her boss to such sexism. "When a woman works closely with her male boss, it's called intimate," Lategano said in 1997. "When a male does the same, it's called loyal." Former South Carolina governor Beasley similarly accused his opponents of "blatant sexism" when they raised questions about his relationship with a key female staffer. Colorado governor Roy Romer also accused prying journalists of "sexism" when he was questioned during his two reelection campaigns about a rumored affair with his deputy chief of staff, B. J. Thornberry. "If B. J. Thornberry had been a man, this issue would never be here," the governor said when the rumor first appeared in print in an alternative newspaper in 1990. "It's one of the problems that women have, I think, in the workplace. How can they be viewed for what they are and what their talents are rather than the fact that they are female." Eight years later, Romer undermined that argument when he confessed to a longstanding "affectionate"—but not "sexual"—extramarital relationship with his former top aide and close adviser. Romer's

1998 admission was prompted by the publication of images from a secretly recorded surveillance video that showed the governor and Thornberry engaged in a six-minute kiss at a Washington, D.C., airport.[15]

Extramarital affairs are not the only romantic/professional relationships that invite scrutiny. Even relationships between unmarried partners can pose potential conflicts, as Kentucky lieutenant governor Steve Henry found out at the start of his losing 1998 Senate bid. As Henry was preparing to launch his campaign for the Democratic nomination in 1997, the *Louisville Courier-Journal* reported that he briefly dated a corrections officer who negotiated a union contract when he was a county commissioner. Henry said there was no link between the relationship and the county contract, which he had voted to approve. "I think it's time we leave people's social lives alone," Henry said. "As lieutenant governor, it would be inappropriate to expect me never to date anyone in state government. My responsibility is to make sure whoever I date has no special advantages or disadvantages because they date me."[16]

Henry's protests aside, workplace relationships involving political figures raise questions that journalists often cannot ignore, including questions about favoritism, harassment and worse. Nonetheless, some discreet office romances escape press attention. Even in the overheated rampage through the private past of members of Congress during the House impeachment debate, few news organizations revisited Clinton defender John Conyers's 1990 marriage to a twenty-five-year-old former intern in his congressional office. The Judiciary Committee's ranking Democrat was a sixty-one-year-old bachelor at the time of the very private wedding. Conyers's new bride had their first child one month later.[17]

The press also ignored House Speaker Newt Gingrich's romance with a House committee aide. The relationship with

Callista Bisek only received widespread attention in the summer of 1999, seven months after Gingrich left office, when a supermarket tabloid staked out the couple's comings and goings in Washington and a Georgia judge ordered the Hill staffer deposed as part of the former Speaker's divorce proceedings. Rumors of the Gingrich–Bisek affair circulated before then. Bisek was identified in a 1995 *Vanity Fair* profile of Gingrich as the Speaker's "favorite breakfast companion," a reference that was repeated at the time in a London newspaper and by *Time* magazine columnist Margaret Carlson. During the impeachment debate last year, the muckraking online magazine *Salon* mentioned "persistent (though unproven) rumors" about a Gingrich affair in a September 1998 article. A few months later, *Hustler* magazine publisher Larry Flynt alluded vaguely to Bisek in the *Flynt Report*, his glossy report about congressional misdeeds, identifying her at the end of a two-page spread on the Speaker as a former congressman's aide.[18]

For a mainstream news organization, taking the story beyond such rumor-mongering would have required an invasive investigation and stakeout, much like the one the *Star* tabloid conducted after Gingrich retired. Despite the *Miami Herald*'s 1987 stakeout of Gary Hart and Donna Rice, most journalists have little appetite for such snooping, even on legitimate stories like the Gingrich–Bisek relationship.

5. Sexual activity that is compulsive and/or manifestly indiscreet, and therefore potentially dangerous.

Republican senator Bob Packwood of Oregon set the standard for this kind of conduct. A thirty-three-month Senate ethics probe, prompted by a 1992 *Washington Post* report, identified almost twenty women who accused the fifth-term lawmaker of inappropriate sexual advances, including sticking his tongue into women's mouths and propositioning one woman for sex.

Packwood apologized for his actions, which he said were "unwelcome and insensitive," but waged a protracted fight to save his job. In September 1995, the Ethics Committee recommended that the Senate expel the senator for sexual and official misconduct. Packwood resigned the next day.[19]

Accusations about Bill Clinton raise similar questions about the president's sex life. The various sins he has acknowledged make him the very personification of compulsive and indiscreet sexual behavior in public office. Yet, in fairness, the evidence supporting some of the accusations against Clinton underscores the difficulties that journalists face in handling such charges. Former Arkansas state employee Paula Jones accused Clinton of luring her to a Little Rock hotel room in 1991, when she says he dropped his pants and requested oral sex. Former White House aide Kathleen E. Willey accused him of groping her during an extended embrace in a hallway near the Oval Office in 1993. Juanita Broaddrick, an Arkansas nursing home operator, said he sexually assaulting her in a hotel room in 1978, when then–state attorney general Clinton was a candidate for governor. The facts in all three cases are somewhat contradictory, inconclusive, and in many ways impossible to prove or disprove. That makes deciding how to fairly present these significant allegations to readers and viewers difficult for news decisionmakers.

In the Broaddrick case, NBC News had the first on-the-record interview with Broaddrick about her charges, but waited until the story appeared in the *Wall Street Journal* and the *Washington Post* to air its account because some top network officials were not satisfied with the level of substantiation. "I kept asking for more information and more cross-checking and more digging, and that takes time," NBC News president Andrew Lack told the *Post*.[20]

Stories about patterns of sexual misconduct impose the same burdens of proof that journalists accept when writing about a single, private sexual relationship or incident. However, the number and type of accusations multiply those burdens. Legal and ethical implications—is the alleged conduct illegal?—are also a consideration for journalists, who are hesitant to print or broadcast de facto editorial indictments. On the other hand, decision-making is easier when the alleged conduct is already the subject of an official investigation, such as an independent counsel or House Judiciary Committee investigation or a Senate Ethics Committee probe. These sorts of inquiries can serve as a news hook for such a story. Fortunately, allegations like those about Packwood and Clinton rarely arise, even in this period of political scandal and private scrutiny. But a 1995 remark by then-senator Alan K. Simpson on the day of Bob Packwood's resignation suggests that this might be a more significant area of investigation than one might hope or expect. "Expelling someone for something that does not even reach the level of sexual harassment is a stunning decision," the Wyoming Republican said. "I looked around that room [the Senate chamber] and saw people who had done things much worse than that."[21]

6. *Any ongoing private behavior that is potentially or actually debilitating, such as alcohol or drug abuse.*

Two months after the *Washington Post* broke the story about Senator Bob Packwood's alleged sexual misconduct, the *Oregonian* newspaper in Portland published a lengthy article documenting the Republican lawmaker's "binge drinking." The newspaper said eleven friends, employees, and family members, including Packwood's ex-wife, thought the senator should seek treatment for his drinking. It also said Packwood's alcohol consumption led to "embarrassing personal situations" and "occasionally interfere[d] with Senate business."[22] Two years later, Packwood himself suggested that his drinking had contributed to his downfall, telling CBS that he drank so heavily at one point in his life that he could not remember many of the alleged incidents of sexual misconduct he was accused of. "That doesn't excuse the conduct," Packwood said, "but I simply can't remember."[23] Coverage of Packwood's heavy drinking before his narrow reelection in 1992 might have headed off the tawdry two-and-a-half-year investigation of the Oregon senator, which consumed much of the Senate's time from 1992 to 1995. But the subject received no attention before the *Post*'s 1992 exposé, even though the senator's drinking habits were apparently well known before the official investigation of his unwelcome sexual advances.

Times are changing for political lushes. Reporters are much more willing to investigate alcohol use than they were in an earlier era, when the press routinely ignored drinking by politicians, even public drunkenness on the floor of the House and Senate. A clear turning point came in 1974, when the House stripped Arkansas Democrat Wilbur Mills of his chairmanship of the Ways and Means Committee after news reports about his drunken adventures with Fanne Foxe, a Washington stripper known as the "Argentine Firecracker." Among Mills's exploits with Foxe: A late-night swim in the Potomac Tidal Basin after police stopped the congressman's car for speeding through Washington without its headlights on, and an inebriated onstage appearance by the congressman at a Boston strip club.[24]

While the Mills story set a precedent that still applies today, journalists are nonetheless just as anxious covering stories about politicians' libations as they are with stories about politicians' libidos. As with stories about sexual indiscretions, the journalistic concern is proof: Minus a Breathalyzer test, a police report, or an on-the-record comment, proving "excessive" drinking is difficult. Cultural questions can also cloud coverage of political drinking. As Democrat Raymond L. Flynn was gearing up to run for Massachusetts governor in 1997, the former Boston mayor and U.S. ambassador to the Vatican accused the *Boston Globe* of an anti–Irish Catholic bias for writing a lengthy story about his drinking habits.

The *Globe* article suggested that Flynn understated both the frequency the and amount of his drinking, but said there was no indication that alcohol affected his public duties. The article also noted that, as mayor, Flynn frequently drank late into the night in Boston pubs, often with *Globe* reporters and editors. The decision to publish and document the longstanding rumors about Flynn's alcohol consumption sparked a journalistic debate. The political editor at the *Boston Herald*, the *Globe*'s rival, and other local reporters and columnists questioned why Flynn was targeted for coverage when former Republican governor William Weld was also known for occasional heavy imbibing. The CBS news show *60 Minutes*, which ran a segment by correspondent Mike Wallace on the *Globe* story, even retrieved file footage of an apparently inebriated Weld slurring his way through his 1995 victory speech.[25] But *Globe* ombudsman Jack Thomas was correct in defending the newspaper against the criticism of readers and veteran journalists who said incidents of Flynn's public drunkenness were not newsworthy:

> [T]he rules have changed. At a time when the public struggles with the damaging effects of alcohol, when teachers worry about drinking among teenagers, when newspapers report carnage because of drunk drivers, and when colleges hold press conferences to explain why students have drunk themselves to death, any newspaper

that ignores a pattern of public drunkenness by a candidate for governor has ethics made of eggshells.[26]

The public apparently sided with the *Globe* in this debate. In a November 1997 poll by the newspaper and WBZ-TV, nearly 60 percent of likely voters surveyed said the media should report instances of public drunkenness involving a gubernatorial hopeful.[27] Flynn eventually abandoned his 1998 bid for governor to run for an open U.S. House seat. He lost the Democratic primary race, his first defeat in a thirty-year career in politics.

7. *Any illegal drug use (whether ongoing or not) that has occurred as an adult, and any incident in the same period in which the candidate has condoned the use of illegal drugs in his or her presence, whether participating or not.*

Many government employees, especially those who serve in sensitive positions requiring a security clearance, must answer standard questions on their job applications about past drug use. Those who apply for work through the voting booth do not have to fill out job applications, but it is reasonable to expect anyone who seeks a position of public trust to answer the same questions that he or she would have to ask potential staff members. Texas governor George W. Bush suggested this standard during the early stages of the Republican presidential race in 1999, when he was refusing to respond to unsubstantiated rumors that he had used cocaine. Initially, Bush said questions about his behavior when he was in his twenties were unfair. "When I was young and irresponsible I was young and irresponsible," he told *Newsweek*. Nine months later, when a journalist asked about the drug-use questions routinely submitted to applicants for senior government jobs, Bush amended his answer, saying he would have met the standards for employment imposed on top officials at any time during his father's term in the White House. Based on President George Bush's initial hiring policy in the 1980s, which ruled out candidates for senior positions who admitted using drugs in the previous fifteen years, his son effectively denied illegal drug use after 1974, when he was twenty-eight.[28]

The standard proposed by George W. Bush has the benefit of being flexible, since it will change with public attitudes and government hiring policies related to past drug use. The White House administration of Bush's father, for example, turned its fifteen-year rule into a ten-year rule after finding that past use of illegal drugs was so common among baby boomers that the original policy eliminated many of the best-qualified candidates for a number of top jobs.[29] By applying the rules imposed on any employee who would report to an officeholder, the Bush standard also ensures that a candidate faces a level of scrutiny that is appropriate to the job he or she is seeking.

Whether Bush's 1999 answer to the drug question met his own standard is debatable. At the time, the federal questionnaire for "national security positions" required applicants to acknowledge any illegal drug use in the past seven years. But the Clinton administration advised those seeking senior government jobs to admit to any illegal drug use since turning eighteen. Answers to these questions are confidential for prospective government workers, but since no agency other than the press—and perhaps one's political enemies—screens prospective elected officials, what level of disclosure should be applied to a candidate?[30]

Voters have shown themselves to be reasonable employers when it comes to questions about substance abuse, which argues for the strictest interpretation of the Bush standard for disclosure. In 1998, Georgia state senator Mark Taylor confirmed that he used marijuana and cocaine while in his twenties after a source sent the *Macon Telegraph* copies of his sealed deposition

from a 1992 custody fight. Taylor's opponents in the 1998 lieutenant governor's race tried to make an issue of his admitted
drug use, which he said ended fifteen years earlier, after he
learned that his wife was pregnant. Despite his rival's snipes—
and a brutal, unsubstantiated television advertisement that suggested he had an ongoing narcotics problem—Taylor prevailed
in the Democratic primary, a runoff vote and the general election that fall.[31]

8. *Any private behavior (whether or not included in the
above categories) that involves the use of public funds or taxpayer-subsidized facilities in a substantial way.*

Abuse of power includes abuse of the perks of power. In
1993, for example, President Clinton denied charges that Arkansas state troopers in his personal security detail helped arrange
sexual liaisons with various women during Clinton's tenure as
governor.[32] Since taxpayers and campaign contributors subsidize
so many aspects of public life, from security and transportation
to meals and phone calls, charges must be "substantial" to justify a significant intrusion into a politician's private life. During the final days of the 1994 governor's race in Colorado, Roy
Romer's Republican challenger accused the incumbent Democrat of using taxpayer funds to make long-distance cellular
phone calls to the home of former top aide B. J. Thornberry, the
woman with whom Romer later acknowledged a longtime "affectionate" relationship. Responding to a flurry of press questions generated by the GOP nominee's veiled, eleventh-hour
swipe in a TV interview, the governor's staff released documents
showing that he had already reimbursed the state for almost all
of the calls. The other calls, spokesmen said, were on official
business, since Thornberry still advised Romer on political and
policy matters, including land use issues she dealt with in a new
post at the Interior Department in Washington, D.C. The tax-

payer's total tab for these phone calls: $18.03. Romer was re-elected by a wide margin the following week.[33]

PRIVATE LIFE SHIELDED FROM PUBLICATION
AND BROADCAST

1. Nonlegal matters involving the candidate's underage children and also other family members, except to the extent that the relatives seek the limelight or influence the official. Also internal family matters, such as child rearing and nonfinancial relationships with relatives and nonpolitical friends.

Spouses, children and other relatives play significant roles in a family member's political career, often serving as surrogate speakers, unofficial advisers and the subjects of speeches, campaign ads and literature. Alma Powell's role in convincing her husband, Colin Powell, not to run for the Republican presidential nomination in 1996 made her a key part of the story about the retired general's decision. But Alma Powell's role also prompted intrusive news reports about her treatment for depression, which the *Philadelphia Inquirer* and *Newsweek* were first to report was among the factors in the family's decision-making.[34]

Reporters often resist such tantalizing stories about political families out of respect for their privacy, even when an elected official or candidate routinely uses family members as props. Journalists often afford political children special protections, although when police caught Vice President Gore's sixteen-year-old daughter, Sarah, in 1995 with an open beer can outside a suburban Washington high school party, the story made national news. In Sarah's case, the Gore family released a statement acknowledging the citation and asking for privacy. That public act made it easier for editors to run with the story. "We were still trying to decide exactly what we were going to do" when the

Gores released their statement, recalled *Washington Post* editor Downie. "Their statement obviously made our decision easier."[35] An erroneous television news report said Gore tried to use her father's name to get out of the citation. When Gore's wife, Tipper, was asked about the incident live on a Fox *Morning News* interview a few days later, she repeated her family's request for privacy: "I would like to say that the fact that my child made a bad error in judgment is on the national news. And not only does she have to deal with the severe disappointment of her family and friends and herself, but she has to deal with the news media's attention, too."[36]

The situation was very different a year later, when rumors swept Washington political circles about why the Gores' son, Albert III, transferred from one prestigious private school to another before eighth grade—a detail that would have no significance beyond a very narrow circle. Many publications assigned reporters to make phone calls and ask questions, but most editors let the story drop. The vice president himself called the Capitol Hill newspaper *Roll Call* to make sure it was not planning a story, and was assured by editor Morton Kondracke that no article was planned:

> We didn't really report the story fully, and he called up. . . . We decided we weren't going to print the story prior to his call. What I should have done was say, "Uh-huh, tell me exactly what happened." But I blurted out, "We're not going to print the story." So he said, "Thank you very much," and hung up and we got nothing out of it. I didn't extract a thing. Exclusive interview and nothing.[37]

The story eventually did seep out in articles in an English newspaper and in the conservative *Weekly Standard* magazine (which did not identify Gore). *Washingtonian* magazine wrote about the incident almost two years later, deep in an article about St. Albans, the school Albert III attended through seventh grade. In a three-paragraph passage, *Washingtonian* reported that the young Gore was suspended before his transfer after he was caught "in possession of substances popular among teen-agers but banned by the school's honor code."[38] Other news-papers and magazines confirmed that the alleged offense involved marijuana but never ran articles about it.

Ann McDaniel, *Newsweek* magazine's managing editor and Washington bureau chief, said the press restraint on the Albert III story was proper, especially in comparison to news reports and commentary about his older sister the year before. "I think that the press was more right on Albert than the daughter," McDaniel said. "We should leave kids alone, unless the parents somehow make it news."[39]

The White House press corps also afforded first daughter Chelsea Clinton tremendous privacy during most of her father's two terms in the White House, despite the Clintons' occasional use of their daughter to offset image problems caused by their troubled marriage. President Clinton and his wife sanctioned news stories about Chelsea's 1997 arrival at Stanford University for her first year of college. But they were furious with tabloid reports about Chelsea's health during her father's impeachment saga, as well as coverage of her breakup with a twenty-year-old boyfriend on the Stanford swimming team. After the president's August 1998 nationally televised speech about his affair with Monica Lewinsky, the first family walked hand-in-hand past TV cameras and news photographers, with Chelsea in the middle, literally holding her family together. Six months after that famous family photo op, however, the Clintons went to great lengths to try to kill a *People* magazine cover story about Chelsea. White House and Secret Service officials called top editors at the magazine to try to spike the February 1999 article, to no avail. But the 1999 story was not Chelsea's first appearance on the magazine's cover. In 1992, the Clintons made a strategic campaign decision to pose with their daughter for a *People* cover photo the same week Clinton accepted his party's nomination. At the time, Clinton's bid for the White House was still endangered by rumors about his infidelities.[40] Mandy Grunwald, the 1992 Clinton campaign's media adviser, explained the couple's decision to pose with Chelsea in an interview a year after the election:

> That was at a point where people really didn't know he had a daughter. And that was because the Clintons are so protective of Chelsea. They didn't want to use her as a prop for the campaign or things that other political families do to their children. But as a result people did not see this side of his life which is so important to him.[41]

Candidates who seek privacy for their families in the press must apply the same standards to their own campaigns. But those who invite journalists into their living room should not be surprised when the press follows them into the bedroom.

A political family's "zone of privacy" only extends as far as the law. In 1994, reporters grilled federal prosecutors in Arizona about whether Cindy McCain, wife of Republican senator John McCain, received special treatment when she was allowed to apply for a diversion program rather than face prosecution for stealing painkillers from a medical charity she headed. The McCains preempted some scrutiny by granting a series of interviews about her two-year addiction to Percocet and Vicodin. The senator's wife attributed her troubles in part to an Ethics Committee investigation of her husband's ties to savings and loan executive Charles H. Keating Jr.[42]

2. *Current extramarital sexual activity as long as it is discreet and noncompulsive, and the official's partner(s) are not connected to his or her public responsibilities and are not minors; in addition, all past sexual activity and personal relationships that occurred many years earlier should not be examined. (Offenses older than a decade might be exempted from scrutiny as a reasonable statute of limitations.)*

Some peccadilloes and past affairs remain out of print and off the air, unless a political enemy makes an on-the-record accusation, a politician makes a public statement or confession, or one of the romantic partners bumbles into another news event. Stories about recent or ongoing relationships, such as President Clinton's affair with Monica Lewinsky, are easier for journalists to justify than stories about past affairs. However, several members of Congress who were vocal critics of the president had their ancient infidelities and secret affairs unearthed because of their statements about Clinton. Congressman Dan Burton preempted a feared but never-published *Vanity Fair* profile in 1998 by confessing to his constituents that he fathered a child out of wedlock with a government employee while he was serving in the Indiana legislature in the 1980s. The canceled *Vanity Fair* story, including allegations of numerous other unconfirmed Burton affairs, was later published by the online magazine *Salon*, which also uncovered Judiciary Committee chairman Henry Hyde's extramarital affair with a married woman in the 1960s. Hyde, who was presiding over the House impeachment hearings, admitted the affair to the cyber-scribes, calling it a "youthful indiscretion" since it happened in the aging lawmaker's forties. After Representative Helen Chenoweth's campaign aired a television advertisement about Clinton's misconduct in the Lewinsky matter, the *Idaho Statesman* published a report about her affair with a married man when she was a single woman in the mid-1980s. Georgia congressman Bob Barr responded publicly to allegations about his messy divorce, court documents from which were reprinted in a glossy anti-impeachment publication produced by *Hustler* magazine publisher Larry Flynt. But Flynt's biggest catch was Bob Livingston, the Speaker-designate from Louisiana, who dramatically resigned from Congress the day of the House impeachment vote after confessing to his colleagues that he had not always been a faithful husband.[43]

Editors and producers might never have found any of these stories newsworthy if members of Congress were not debating perjury charges related to the president's philandering. In fact, many of these stories were well known among journalists but never reported before the Monica Lewinsky investigation came before the House. In addition, decision-makers in most mainstream news organizations only ran stories about the abovementioned admissions and allegations after each member was forced to publicly address the charge, while numerous other accusations about various members of Congress who held their tongues were never reported at all during the same period.

Once revealed—either by journalists or by repentant politicians—sexual affairs and past philandering are like political herpes, frequently flaring up as routine topics for questioning in subsequent profiles and interviews. In *The Nightingale's Song*, a 1995 book about the Vietnam War's effects on five prominent Naval Academy graduates, reporter Robert Timberg described how Senator John McCain's womanizing contributed to the breakup of his first marriage in 1980. At the time, McCain took full responsibility for his role in the divorce, as he did later, in numerous interviews early in the 2000 presidential campaign. But no matter how many times McCain told journalists that he would not discuss the issue in any greater detail than he already had, reporters repeated the same question in interview after interview and profile after profile.[44]

When it comes to stories out of a politician's past, news organizations are often surprisingly happy to be scooped—although that doesn't discourage them from doing follow-up stories of their own. That was the case with McCain's friend, former Senate majority leader Bob Dole, who faced questions about alleged infidelities after his abrupt 1972 divorce. After Dole won the 1996 GOP presidential nomination, a Washington-area woman confirmed to the *Washington Post*, *Time* magazine, and other publications that she had an extramarital affair with Dole that began several years before the breakup of his first marriage. Most news organizations did not report the information to readers and viewers until late in the election year, after the *New York Daily News* ran a story confirming the affair. *Post* executive editor Leonard Downie Jr. said at the time that Dole's long-ago romance did not initially "meet our standards for the publication of information about the private lives of public officials." But, Downie added, "we recognized that our initial decision about publication could be overtaken by events if another news organization published a story that created wide public interest."[45]

3. Sexual orientation per se.

For political reasons and for personal reasons, some politicians prefer to keep their sexual orientation or preference to themselves, posing a difficult question to those assigned to cover them: When is sexuality a legitimate issue? Republican two-term congressman Michael Huffington was asked during his unsuccessful 1994 Senate race about rumors that he was gay. But he did not publicly acknowledge his homosexuality until a January 1999 *Esquire* magazine profile, more than a year after his divorce from conservative commentator Arianna Huffington.[46] Jim Kolbe, another divorced Republican congressman, confirmed long-circulating rumors that he was gay in 1996 only after he learned that the *Advocate*, a national gay newspaper, planned to write a story "outing" him. The *Advocate*'s justification for its reporting was the Arizona congressman's July 1996 vote for a GOP bill allowing states to refuse to sanction homosexual marriages. Kolbe's homosexuality was long rumored. But *Arizona Daily Star* editor Stephen E. Auslander said his newspaper and other news organizations in the state did not report on Kolbe's sexuality before he discussed it publicly because the issue had no bearing on how he did his job. "Public figures have a moral, if not legal, right to privacy. So long as his private life didn't affect his job, it's his own business." Voters in Kolbe's district apparently agreed, reelecting the Tucson-area lawmaker to a seventh term.[47]

Once raised publicly, a question about a politician's sexuality can have an especially long shelf life. Rumors that Republican congressman John Kasich of Ohio was gay started during the House Budget Committee chairman's 1996 reelection campaign and lasted through his brief run for his party's 2000 presidential nomination. In the 1996 race, Kasich's Democratic rival sought a Justice Department investigation of the congressman, alleging a conflict of interest because he shared the lease on a Washington-area townhouse with his well-paid male chief of staff. Kasich, who was divorced at the time, accused his opponent of trying to smear him with an unspoken suggestion of homosexuality. Local media chided the Democrat, but the homosexuality rumor nevertheless got national attention that fall in a *Time* magazine story. After that, the rumor became part of Kasich's journalistic background. A December 1996 gossip item in the *Washington Post* about Kasich's engagement to his second wife snidely asked if he and his aide would continue sharing their townhouse in Alexandria, Virginia, now that the congressman was getting hitched. While the item made no mention of the rumor about Kasich, the reference was clear to politically savvy readers.⁴⁸

4. Drug *or alcohol abuse that was a youthful indulgence or experimentation; also adult abuse at least a decade old, when the individual has fully recovered and clearly abandoned the harmful practices.*

Politicians often defuse potential time bombs in their past by granting confessional interviews, as George W. Bush did when the issue of his drinking came up during the first stages of his White House bid in 2000. He, his wife, and their friends and family discussed the Texas governor's 1986 decision to give up drinking in numerous pre–election-year interviews and profiles. The stories described Bush as a heavy binge drinker. Bush and other sources disagreed about whether his drinking amounted to an alcohol problem, but all agreed the issue was behind him. That's a far cry from the situations involving heavy drinking by those currently in or seeking office described earlier.⁴⁹

Numerous politicians have likewise admitted experimenting with marijuana, most famously candidate Bill Clinton, who as late-night comedians will always remind us, "didn't inhale." Clinton's parsing of his marijuana answers over many years drew more attention than his actual misdeed, which was hardly surprising for a baby boomer who had attended college and graduate school in the late 1960s and early 1970s. During his last campaign for governor of Arkansas in 1990, Clinton said he "never violated the drug laws of the state." Clinton more or less stood by that answer until a televised debate during the Democratic presidential primaries in 1992, when he said he tried marijuana "a time or two" while he was a Rhodes scholar in England in 1968 and 1969. "And I didn't like it, and I didn't inhale and I didn't try it again." Clinton's answer became more of a story than his admission justified because of his evasive and legalistic answers to earlier questions—a problem that would haunt Clinton throughout his presidency. In contrast, during the previous presidential race in 1988, journalists quickly moved on to other matters after reporting that Democratic candidates Al Gore and Bruce Babbitt had tried pot when they were in their twenties. Both candidates, along with Republican congressman Newt Gingrich and other political leaders, came clean about their youthful experiments after questions about past marijuana use sank federal judge Douglas Ginsburg's Supreme Court nomination in 1987. Ginsburg said he had used marijuana with students while he was an adult Harvard Law School professor. That Ginsburg was teaching the law that he was tapped to interpret on the nation's highest court made his otherwise minor admission of law-breaking more significant than that of Gore, Babbitt and Gingrich. (Four years later, Clarence Thomas's admission of past marijuana use when he was young was not an issue in his confirmation as a Supreme Court justice.)

In a contemporary campaign, an indulgence from a candidate's past might not even come up, except in passing, unless the candidate denied it or refused to answer the question, or the issue of alcohol or drug abuse was somehow prominent in the campaign. A political enemy might raise the issue, obliging reporters to follow up. But the campaigns of those who have tried to use such relatively insignificant details against their rivals have generally gone up in smoke. In the 1990 Democratic gubernatorial primary in Texas, Ann Richards's rival accused her of using marijuana and cocaine. Richards, who said she was a recovering alcoholic, refused to respond to the drug accusations, which of course meant that many believed the charges were true. The charges nevertheless backfired when Texas newspapers reported that witnesses accused Richards's opponent of using marijuana in the 1970s. A few days later, Richards won the primary and eventually the governorship. Four years later, former binge-drinker Bush bested her in a campaign in which neither candidate's past drinking was an issue.[50]

WIGGLE ROOM

As mentioned earlier in this chapter, none of the behavior described above should be considered a disqualifying characteristic for public office. Voters must decide when a candidate's behavior violates the public trust based on the offense and the demands of the position to which a politician aspires. This "fairness doctrine" is intended to serve only as a guideline to help journalists and their customers decide when information may be relevant, not to produce decision-making rules or formulas. The "fairness doctrine" also provides a guidepost for the analysis of the issues and case studies discussed throughout the rest of this book.

Standards of conduct and decency vary widely from community to community, and often from political party to political party. Certain conduct might be an issue in a party primary fight but not in a general election contest, or vice versa. In addition, voters hold candidates for different offices accountable for their actions to different degrees. Scrutiny ought to be greatest for presidential and vice presidential candidates, with few exceptions. Holding a candidate for county council or other low-level office to the same standards one might apply to a candidate for the White House is unfair and unrealistic. However, the potential for corruption among officeholders, elected or not, with direct power over schools, roads, or hundreds of state and local employees is often too easily overlooked by journalists hunting for big game or worried about alienating local friends and sources.

A candidate's degree of hypocrisy and lying is often a factor for editors deciding when private conduct is newsworthy. For example, Georgia gubernatorial candidate Mike Bowers legitimized the adultery issue in large part with his strong backing of state sex laws as state attorney general. In court, Bowers successfully defended his office's decision to withdraw a job offer to a young attorney because her planned unofficial union with a lesbian partner would make it hard to uphold "the law of marriage in this state," where fornication and adultery were still misdemeanors. Bowers also successfully defended Georgia's sodomy laws in front of the U.S. Supreme Court. Both positions made him popular with his state's influential Christian conservatives and a legitimate target for private scrutiny.

Glaring political hypocrisy deserves public and media attention. However, hypocrisy is also highly subjective. While some found the past affairs of some of President Clinton's congressional critics to be the height of hypocrisy, others drew distinctions between purely private sexual relationships and one that was the subject of a civil lawsuit and a yearlong criminal probe. Accusations of hypocrisy are usually best left not to the press but to voters and rival political camps to identify and sort out.

One standard that journalists must apply to their reporting on the private lives of political leaders is that every charge printed or aired should be proven or accompanied by a substantial body of evidence. Sorting fact from fiction, evidence from innuendo, is a vital journalistic function at a time when increased competition among different media sources is giving campaign gossip and rumor broader circulation than in the past. The case studies examined in this book include many unsubstantiated rumors, some true, some not. Almost all of these rumors were published or broadcast in some form, usually on TV or radio talk shows or on Internet scandal sheets, such as the *Drudge Report,* before eventually finding their way into the mainstream press. The reporting on rumors examined in this book includes completely unsubstantiated but widely circulated allegations that a prominent young congressional leader retired in 1998 because of a homosexual affair with a Capitol Hill journalist and that President Clinton had an out-of-wedlock child with a prostitute. Our case studies also include rumors such as the existence of Monica Lewinsky's semen-stained dress, which eventually proved to be true but was widely reported—and even incorrectly debunked—before there was sufficient sourcing for the public to judge the value of the information. Some editors believe ignoring such tidbits reflects a news organization's responsible assessment of the facts and underlying evidence. Others believe that rumors themselves can be newsworthy simply because they are "out there," circulating among the public or in political circles, or because a politician feels compelled to issue a denial.

Rumors that journalists print or broadcast must be accompanied by significant reporting on the facts of the matter, as well as information about the source of the gossip. In a multimedia age, any other approach is unfair to political figures, a disservice to readers and viewers, and dangerous for the mainstream media's long-term credibility and viability.

2

Motive

The editors of *Roll Call*, a Capitol Hill newspaper, had a hell of a scoop. Bob Livingston, a Republican congressman from Louisiana and Speaker-designate of the House of Representatives, was confiding in his fellow congressional leaders that he cheated on his wife. Investigative pornographer Larry Flynt, the *Hustler* magazine publisher, was making inquiries based on responses to his full-page ad in the *Washington Post* offering former political paramours big money for their stories. As the full House was preparing to debate articles of impeachment against President Clinton, Livingston was telling his GOP colleagues in a closed-door session that he was prepared to resign before even officially taking his new post.

Roll Call apparently had the whole story to itself. But not for long. It was a Thursday evening in December 1998, and with the newspaper's twice-weekly publishing schedule, another news organization would surely sniff out the scandal before *Roll Call's* next opportunity to get its scoop into print. Instead of waiting four days until its Monday issue, *Roll Call* published the article that night on the newspaper's Web site. Reporters and editors also called colleagues in other newsrooms to alert them about the story before Livingston issued the written statement that he gave to the small-circulation political newspaper as a general news release.

To executive editor Morton M. Kondracke, the decision to break the Livingston story online was an easy one. "The sourcing was impeccable on the basic facts of the story, and when Livingston came through on the statement, it was a no-brainer. It was an important story." Kondracke went on Fox News Channel to break the story shortly before his staff posted their online extra on the Internet.[1]

Roll Call's cyber-scoop shows how new technologies and competitive forces have turned the pressure cooker of daily news decisions into a microwave oven, especially when it comes to sensational and sensitive stories about the private lives of political figures. Decisions over which a newsroom might have deliberated for weeks are sometimes made in minutes—or even instantly on the proliferating television and talk radio programs that help fill airtime on a growing number of news channels. Editors who hesitate run the risk of having their decisions made for them by rivals. In the most famous instance of this reverse editing process, online gossip Matt Drudge reported in January 1998 that *Newsweek* magazine spiked a story at the last moment about independent counsel Kenneth W. Starr's investigation of President Clinton's sexual relationship with a White House intern. The item on *Newsweek*'s nonstory on the *Drudge Report*, a three-year-old Web site and virtual gossip sheet, was the subject of talk show speculation even before the *Washington Post*, ABC News and *Los Angeles Times* did the first actual news reports on the Monica Lewinsky story. On ABC that Sunday, four days before the network's first news story on Lewinsky, conservative commentator Bill Kristol brought up the Drudge item on the Sunday morning show *This Week*. During a discussion of Clinton's closed-door deposition in the Paula Jones lawsuit the previous day, Kristol told the ABC show's more than 3 million viewers that "the story in Washington this morning is that *Newsweek* magazine was going to go with a big story based on tape-recorded conversations" with a "a summer intern" in the office of former White House chief of staff Leon Panetta. "It's going to be a question of whether the media is now going to report what are pretty well-validated charges of presidential behavior in the White House," Kristol said. Cohost Sam Donaldson quickly changed the subject: "I'm not an apologist for *Newsweek*, but if their editors decided they didn't have it cold enough to go with, I don't think that we can here without—unless you've seen what they were basing their decision on—how could we say *Newsweek* was wrong to kill it."[2] But by then it was too late. ABC's televised exchange on *Newsweek*'s editorial decision *not* to run a story was now news to an audience bigger than the magazine's paid U.S. circulation of 3.2 million—and on the day before the newsweekly's story would have been available to its readers, had it actually run the Lewinsky article.

That *Newsweek* initially resisted publishing its Lewinsky story, despite the knowledge that the news would almost certainly break in other outlets before the magazine's next issue, is somewhat comforting. Competitive considerations clearly do not overwhelm all editorial decisions, even with the growing pressures of twenty-four-hours-a-day news online and on cable television. Ann McDaniel, *Newsweek*'s managing editor and Washington bureau chief, said she and her colleagues knew they would be scooped:

> When we didn't publish Monica the first weekend, we knew there was no chance that in the seven days that followed somebody would not break the story. But it did not meet our standards and we chose not to publish. It was an extraordinarily difficult decision. We like to be first. But

we like more to be accurate. Once we had agreed that it did not meet our standards, we felt terrible, but we couldn't do anything about it. We weren't going to violate our standards just to get out there with it.[3]

Such decisions are rare. Intensifying competitive forces often drive news choies, and lead to some editorial errors, as was the case with the *Dallas Morning News* and the *Wall Street Journal*, each of which retracted news stories published online before the newspaper's normal deadlines early in the Lewinsky probe. However, editorial errors are not unique to online publishing or cable news stations, as most newspapers demonstrate in their daily correction boxes. The modern, technology-driven editorial arms race only magnifies dangers that competition among traditional news media always posed:

- Judgment is sacrificed: Decisions made in response to stories by other news organizations are not always based on a news organization's own standards or usual deliberative practices.
- Incremental developments are emphasized: Fear of being scooped or the desire to find a fresh angle on a story broken by a competitor can unduly elevate a marginal news story.
- New standards are set by the least common denominator: Even bad journalism—a poorly sourced accusation, an unsubstantiated rumor—can generate a denial or statement by a politician or his or her enemies that will turn an otherwise questionable story into news that other editors cannot realistically ignore.

Competition and the other forces that drive the press coverage of private political behavior are neither new nor entirely unhealthy. Many of these forces are tied to Watergate. The effect of journalism's role in ousting the thirty-seventh president still is still felt in newsrooms full of eager reporters and grizzled editors, many of whom were inspired to pursue their careers by Bob Woodward and Carl Bernstein's exploits in *All the President's Men*. The public's cynicism about political figures since Richard Nixon's resignation in 1974 is shared by many of those who cover politics, creating a feedback loop in which journalistic skepticism and the public's distrust amplify and distort one another. The role of a candidate's "character" as a defining issue in contemporary politics is yet another Watergate legacy, the importance of which has grown as the press has replaced the political parties as the unofficial candidate "screening committee." Other institutional changes have also affected journalistic attitudes about the private lives of political figures. The growing number of women in newsrooms over the past three decades, for instance, demolished old-boy networks that allowed reporters to wink and ignore certain behavior they observed among politicians, as they did among their colleagues. Changing legal standards gave journalists more leeway to pry into areas that might have been risky before 1964, when a Supreme Court decision changed libel standards to require a public official to show "actual malice" to prove that a statement was defamatory. Editorial standards have changed, too. News stories about the "distinguishing characteristics" of President Clinton's penis or his use of cigars as sex toys would have been almost unimaginable in 1933, when the *Washington Post*'s new owner, Eugene Meyer, decreed that his newspaper would be "fit reading for the young as well as the old." While a plaque in the *Post*'s lobby still pronounces Meyer's principles, his newspaper reflects more contemporary tastes and standards, which also allow partial nudity and increasing use of profanity on prime-time television. The news that is fit to print, to paraphrase the motto of the *New York Times*, is clearly a moving target.[4]

While these profound changes in the role and character of newsrooms have been affecting journalism for many years, new forces are creating powerful and sometimes irresistible pressures on editors. Information technologies are changing the way news is reported and circulated. Growing competition from nontraditional news sources is also a wild card in the editorial process. These developments present unique threats to journalists' credibility as well as to the privacy of political personalities.

NEW INFORMATION TECHNOLOGY

In *All the President's Men*, Carl Bernstein and Bob Woodward recount the arduous, low-tech process of tracking down Kenneth H. Dahlberg, the Midwest finance chairman for the Committee to Reelect the President, whose name appeared on a $25,000 check deposited in the bank account of one of the Watergate burglars. Woodward, following up on a lead phoned in by Bernstein in Florida, worked his telephone from the *Washington Post* newsroom, while the newspaper's librarians scoured files full of news clippings and photos in search of any information on the elusive Dahlberg. After much digging, a photo caption on a picture prompted Woodward to try his luck with local information in Minneapolis. While Woodward's hunch produced a current home telephone number for the surprised Dahlberg, the young *Post* reporters' first big break in the Watergate story is also a reminder of how much the tools of journalism have changed since 1972.[5]

Almost three decades later, reporters track down possible sources with technologies that would have made Woodward and

Bernstein's job much easier than it was when Deep Throat met reporters in garages rather than send encrypted messages from Internet "remailers." The phone number for a campaign fundraiser such as Dahlberg is usually available from one of the telephone companies' national directory services for a small fee, or for free on the Internet from one of the numerous online "White Page" directories offered by Yahoo! and other major Web sites. If not, any reporter with access to the Web would surely find a lead in one of the campaign committee's own documents, many of which are now published electronically on the Federal Election Commission (FEC) Web site. Campaign documents published online by the FEC also include the names, addresses and usually the place of employment for most contributors to federal campaigns, the national political parties, and political action committees, or PACs.[6]

As the Internet becomes an increasingly important tool for individuals and organizations to share and distribute information, it is also becoming an invaluable tool for journalists trolling for information on those with personal ties to political figures. With growing Internet access and familiarity in newsrooms, a politician's college roommates, former lovers, drinking buddies, and business partners are often as close as a reporter's keyboard and monitor. Reporters covering Newt Gingrich's divorce in the summer of 1999, for instance, could find congressional aide Callista Bisek's direct telephone number in the online version of the *Congressional Directory* published by the Government Printing Office. Bisek's e-mail address at the House Agriculture Committee, where she worked as a scheduler, was also available on the Web from the "Alumni E-mail Database" at Luther College in Decorah, Iowa, where her contact information was listed along with that of other members of the class of 1988. Her e-mail address was also on the Web page for the City of Fairfax Band, with whom she volunteered in the horn section. Searches on free Internet "people finders" turned up Bisek's phone number and home address and even offered maps and directions. Such details, including one's activities and affiliations, are essential for journalists in the early stages of reporting, before a previously unknown person is suddenly catapulted into the center of a national news story. However, journalists must also determine the reliability of any information obtained from an Internet site, especially one that does not have an official affiliation. Information retrieved from pure Internet sources is also often fleeting. Some details about Bisek, for example, were yanked from the Web in the weeks after the news of her relationship with Gingrich first appeared.

Reporters digging into the personal life of a political figure can also unearth information on digital information services such as Reed Elsevier Inc.'s LEXIS-NEXIS and Dow Jones Interactive. Both proprietary computer services—which are also used by lawyers, private detectives, business developers and others—archive articles, news stories, wire reports and transcripts from thousands of news sources. Other news organizations, including the Knight-Ridder publishing company, offer their own online news archives, from which customers can retrieve stories for a small fee. Falling prices in response to competition from online editions of many newspapers, magazines and TV news operations are increasing newsrooms' access to these searchable gold mines, which offer not just a wealth of information on politicians but also the sources who might have information about public figures. Computer research services provide easy access to past profiles of a politician and his or her previous public statements on a topic, some of which might cause personal or political embarrassment. Online news archives are also the fastest way for journalists to excavate personal charges or accusations that a political enemy might have raised in a past campaign or political fight, the details of which these research services almost guarantee will be repeated in future news accounts.

Electronic news archives can serve as a newsroom's institutional memory, adding quotes, facts and context to stories that might otherwise be hard to retrieve. Journalists increasingly depend on computer services such as LEXIS-NEXIS to jump-start their reporting. But few of these reporters are familiar with the serious limitations and even dangers of relying too heavily on articles retrieved from computer searches. A fruitless search may only mean that a key publication is not available, as is the case with a number of state and local newspapers as well as publications from certain chains. In addition, articles from a particular news organization may be available only on one service or another, requiring thorough journalists to pay for multiple searches to be sure they get the whole story. Even then, reporters must ensure that there are not other leads and sources they are missing because they did not turn up in a computer search. A badly constructed search might miss a critical detail, such as a follow-up story amending or retracting a key detail. A search that turns up news of a lawsuit or an arrest, for instance, might miss a later story that says the case was dismissed. Reporters also need to know whether the version of a story they are examining is in fact correct. Television transcripts published online are often uncorrected early drafts, which sometimes misattribute statements or contain other errors. Some newspapers archive electronic versions of their stories that leave out fixes and additions made by copy editors in the later editions of the publication. Other publications, especially magazines, are "scanned" into an electronic format to make them searchable, an imprecise process in which a computer converts images of letters and numbers on a page into actual text. (Scanning might; for example, convert "Bill Bradley" to "8i11 8rad1ey.") Other articles are retyped from scratch, a process that can introduce other errors. The level of human intervention and editing in the scanning and retyping process, which is often unknown to a search service client, can greatly affect the reliability of an article retrieved online. Bruce William Oakley, editor of the online edition of the *Arkansas Democrat-Gazette* in Little Rock, detailed many such problems—including inaccurate headlines, bylines, and page numbers—during a four-month study funded by the John S. and James L. Knight Foundation. Oakley detailed the discrepancies he found between the print and electronically archived versions of front-page newspaper stories in a March 1998 article in the *Columbia Journalism Review*, which is available online from the Dow Jones Interactive (DJI) "Publications Library." Ironically, the massive number of typographical errors in the electronic version of Oakley's article demonstrates the pitfalls of relying on the results of computer searches. The DJI version of the story began this way:

> John Brummett knnw he'd made a mistake, and now it was stardng him in tte face. Brummett, a political columnds at thn Arkansas Democrat-Gazette in Little Rock, couldn't let ttis error get publdshed. Hn tad written ttat a publdc figure served time, when in fact the convictdon was overturned and thn man tad never been behind bars durdng his appeal.[7]

Typographical errors of this sort in the spelling of a name can make an important story impossible to locate by computer search. At the same time, typographical and even factual errors in the original text of an article are often perpetuated in an electronic archive, where they can be retrieved and repeated by others.

The story of the Gingrich–Bisek relationship, which earlier demonstrated the power and limits of new Internet tools for reporters researching a story, also shows the limits of searching proprietary online information services. A computer-savvy journalist looking for information on Callista Bisek in LEXIS-NEXIS or Dow Jones Interactive before her relationship with Newt Gingrich made headlines would have found few references to her before the former House Speaker's 1999 divorce. A search of either service might have turned up a passing reference in a London newspaper in August 1995, but probably would have missed a similar passage that same month in a Margaret Carlson column in *Time* magazine. While the *Time* story was available electronically, Bisek's first and last names were both misspelled: "Calista Bistek."[8] At the same time, neither LEXIS-NEXIS nor DJI offered the full text of the one article that prompted both mentions—a September 1995 *Vanity Fair* profile of Gingrich, which identified Bisek as the Speaker's "favorite breakfast companion." A computer-dependent reporter also might have missed a reference to Bisek in the 1999 *Flynt Report*, seven months before Gingrich filed for divorce. The text of the article was not available from LEXIS-NEXIS or DJI, and even if it had been, the article referred to her only as a "female staff member of then-Congressman Steve Gunderson (R-Wisconsin)." A reporter would have had to go back to a 1994 congressional staff directory to determine that Bisek had worked for Gunderson as an executive assistant before she worked for the House Agriculture Committee, where she served during her relationship with the Speaker.[9]

Limitations aside, the power and importance of new information technologies is not lost on the professional spinners who manage the public image of political figures. In 1999, Republican presidential candidate George W. Bush waged a public fight against gwbush.com, a spoofy, campaign-like Web site produced by a twenty-nine-year-old online heckler to distribute damaging news and gossip about the real candidate. While helping to publicize the critical Web site, the Bush team also publicly rebutted its charges and called attention to the fact that it was not the official campaign site, georgewbush.com, as it first appeared. The Bush camp also buttressed its online defenses by buying Web addresses for other site names, such as bushsucks.com and bushblows.com.[10] At the Clinton White House, special counsel Lanny J. Davis selectively leaked damaging information to certain reporters in an effort not just to control how the story played in the press, but to ensure that the administration's spin on the news would turn up prominently in computer searches. As Davis explained in a 1999 kiss-and-tell account of his time masterminding White House damage control, a selective leak created a "predicate story" that became "the foundation block for all other reporters and for all future reporting":

> [The predicate story] will pop up in every Lexis-Nexis database search from then on. If it is complete and accurate, it will likely kill or at least diminish follow-up stories, since there won't be much more to report. If it is incomplete and wrong, then the Lexis database will cause it to repeat and grow, like a virus, more and more difficult to catch up with, correct, and cure.[11]

If the White House and White House candidates are paying this much attention to how reporters gather and use electronic information, editors and reporters must be just as thoughtful—and even more cautious.

ALTERNATIVE NEWS SOURCES

Traditional media organizations are no longer the sole gateways of information on those seeking or holding political office. At the same time, changes in the focus and distribution of the news give local publications surprising influence, while large national media organizations are increasingly playing a role in state and local politics. The role that alternative local newspapers, national media outlets and Internet-only news sources played in recent political controversies shows some of the effects of these nontraditional information channels.

Alternative Newspapers

Distributed at coffeehouses, restaurants, bookstores, and nightclubs, the free alternative newspapers available in most major media markets reach a young and politically engaged readership. These mostly advertiser-supported weekly or monthly publications also have small editorial staffs, armies of freelance contributors, and news standards that are sometimes far less scrupulous than mainstream news organizations, even with the traditional media's many shortcomings. Political rumors—often well circulated, but rarely published to a mass audience—easily find their way into print in alternative newspapers, sometimes in the name of exposing hypocrisy or prying open the mainstream media's lock on information and knowledge. That the rumors often prove true does not excuse shoddy, poorly sourced journalism.

- In Colorado, Denver's *Westword* weekly first printed rumors about Governor Roy Romer's then-alleged relationship with a top aide in a 1990 article on how the gossip was affecting the rest of the state political establishment.[12] The article offered no on-the-record proof of

the relationship, which Romer later admitted. But
Romer's public denials of the *Westword* story gave the
national news magazine *Insight* reason to revisit the issue almost eight years later, when it published a private
investigator's photos of Romer and his aide kissing in an
airport parking lot.

- In South Carolina, a Columbia monthly called the *Point*
printed a short, unconfirmed item suggesting that Governor David Beasley's wife had left him after she pushed
her way past his security guards to catch him in a compromising situation with his female communications
director. Other South Carolina news organizations investigated but could not substantiate the rumors about a
Beasley affair and breakup; many of the rumors in fact
proved untrue. But rumors first published in the *Point*
in 1996 reemerged as a campaign issue in the governor's
failing bid for a second term two years later.[13]

- In Indiana, the *Nuvo* weekly in Indianapolis wrote about
U.S. Representative Dan Burton's rumored womanizing
weeks before investigations by other media organizations
led the Republican congressman to publicly confess that
he fathered a child out of wedlock with a government
employee in the early 1980s. A 1998 editorial by *Nuvo*
editor Harrison Ullmann said Burton "had a reputation
for sex with convenient women that was at least as aw-
ful and awesome as the Clinton reputation," and asked
the lawmaker to answer a series of detailed questions
about his sex life. That August, when Burton warned his
constituents to brace for more media reports about his
personal life, the *Indianapolis Star-News* cited Ullmann's
then-unsubstantiated editorial.[14]

- In New York, a lengthy Buffalo *Beat* editorial detailed
completely unsubstantiated allegations about retiring

representative Bill Paxon. The year-old newsweekly suggested Paxon was forced to retire in early 1998 because a political enemy threatened to expose the congressman's unproven homosexual, extramarital relationship with a Capitol Hill reporter. Paxon's on-the-record denials of the *Beat* story on a Buffalo-area radio talk show were repeated in subsequent profiles and interviews with the congressman in the *Washington Post*, the *Washington Times* and the *Boston Globe*.[15]

The Paxon example perhaps best illustrates the power of a free, relatively small-circulation alternative newspaper to influence the coverage of a story about a national political figure. Prior to its publication in the *Beat*, only a small gossip item in the *Jerusalem Post* hinted at the rumors about Paxon's unexpected departure from Congress. Some members of the House and many journalists doubted Paxon's stated reason for retiring—to spend time with his wife, former Staten Island congresswoman Susan Molinari, and their baby daughter. News reports and commentary about Paxon's decision were filled with oblique references to other unstated factors, including speculation that he was the victim of a smear campaign tied to his widely expected challenge of House Majority Leader Dick Armey. But while dark rumors about Paxon circulated quickly and widely on Capitol Hill and in New York, most news organizations found no credible substantiation to justify running stories about the nature of the gossip. John Yang, who was political editor for the *Washington Post*'s Style section at the time, said the decision not to publish the rumor "wasn't even a close call. We decided to report it out, but we weren't going to print it. . . . It had no credibility."[16]

Editors at the Buffalo *Beat* had a different take. In fact, press inquiries about the rumors served as a news hook for a

Beat article that said "reporters all over the country" were look-ing for evidence of a "more-than-professional relationship" be-tween Paxon and a Washington journalist, who committed sui-cide three days before the congressman announced his plans. (All accounts from the journalist's friends and colleagues that we have obtained supported Paxon's denials of the rumors, and they unequivocally pointed to other unrelated factors as the causes for this tragic suicide.)[17] Paxon angrily denied these "absolutely libelous" allegations in an on-air exchange after the *Beat* story became a topic of discussion on Buffalo radio station WGR:

> You had plenty of time to check out the facts. You have a responsibility to check out rumors as fact. This is what I've been subjected to, and thank God every credible news organization— even the *Buffalo News*, which has been no fan of mine over the years—has chosen not to run this because there isn't a single bit of truth in it.[18]

The *Buffalo News* wrote a story about Paxon's on-air de-nial, detailing the rumors about him in its very next edition. With that, the print circulation of the Paxon gossip went from 45,000 in the *Beat* to 240,000 in the *News*—and eventually even greater distribution as the congressman's denial was repeated in stories by other news organizations.[19]

The Paxon story was a big news coup for a little newspa-per. But in an e-mail exchange with the authors more than a year after her controversial article, *Beat* editor Natalie Green said she would not have published the same story she wrote "with the benefit of hindsight," even though it called attention to her young newspaper.

> I'd have structured the editorial differently so that rumor-mongering wasn't the focal point of

the piece, perhaps included less shocking details, and instead emphasized the political maneuvering. What we lacked in experience we made up for in guts, though I had no idea whatsoever we'd get the attention we did at the time as a year-old, 45,000-circulation alternative weekly. Locally, we were accused of doing it as an attention-getting device, but I did and do still believe that Paxon was likely driven out of office by Newt Gingrich and Dick Armey because he challenged their power, and that was worth editorializing about.[20]

There may in fact have been a legitimate news story in identifying the source of the hurtful gossip about Paxon and the young journalist, who had written particularly damning stories about House Majority Leader Armey and other members of the GOP's congressional leadership before his suicide. Journalists who investigated the story could not track the rumor back to its source. Some sources suggested the gossip originated with Armey's staff, but other evidence suggested Armey's enemies, including top Democrats, circulated the rumors to damage the majority leader. Ultimately, the allegations were so widespread in the Capitol that the point of origin may never be known.

Out-of-Market Publications

The personal foibles of state and municipal politicians are often well known to local journalists. But writers for national publications, not local ones, often end up breaking news about a politician's personal behavior to his or her constituents. Several factors contribute to this almost federalist approach to political scandal. An out-of-town or out-of-state editor may see a candidate's private affairs in a different context than a newsroom counterpart closer to home—perhaps linking a story about a politician's routine marital problems to a similar situation involving a candidate for higher office or in another part of the country. An old news story or gossipy tidbit about a political figure that is ancient history to the politician's constituents may still be an interesting revelation to the readers of a national publication. In addition, reporters and editors at a hometown newspaper or TV newsroom sometimes have close, if not friendly, relationships with political figures in their circulation and broadcast areas, especially compared to a national journalist who parachutes into town for a tactical assault.

By 1998, Governor Roy Romer's long-rumored relationship with a top aide was old news in Colorado political circles. But Romer's role as the Democratic National Committee's general chairman during the early stages of the Monica Lewinsky investigation renewed the national news magazine *Insight*'s interest in the old, much-denied gossip. Paul M. Rodriguez, the *Insight* managing editor who wrote the magazine's February 1998 story on Romer, obtained material from private investigators, apparently paid for by Romer's political enemies in Colorado, which detailed intimate extramarital moments between the governor and his former deputy chief of staff. Among the material was a surveillance videotape that showed the couple engaged in long kiss in the parking lot of a Washington, D.C., airport. While not revealing his sources, Rodriguez said news organizations in Colorado could have obtained the same private investigators' reports and other corroborating material on which he based his story, if they had wanted to:

> We tend to forget that there are close relationships that do affect coverage, I guess particularly here in Washington where we assume that everybody beats the bejesus out of everybody. . . . The Romer story should have been explored in great

depth and far sooner than it was. And I found it just amazing when I went into the archives of the [Colorado] newspapers and saw how they short-shrifted and otherwise brushed aside what I thought originally were significant questions.[21]

That neither the *Denver Post* nor the *Rocky Mountain News* obtained and published the investigators' material before *Insight* did was surprising given the rival Denver newspapers' intense competition for news and readers. *Denver Post* editor Dennis Britton, who came to the newspaper two years before *Insight*'s Romer story, said he only learned about the investigators' material after Rodriguez wrote his article. Looking back, Britton said he wished his newspaper had pursued the previously published rumors about a Romer affair more thoroughly when they surfaced in the governor's 1990 and 1994 reelection campaigns, not during his last year in office after an out-of-state publication broke the news first.

One of the things that you have to keep in mind when you think about this is how small the state of Colorado is. This is a state where it's not unusual for people to know the governor. It's absolutely not unusual for reporters to know a governor well. I think there was a distaste for doing it. . . . These stories shouldn't come from another market; they should come from your own market. There's lots of reasons why, not just the competitive reason. The real reason as far as I'm concerned as an editor, is if your staff is in bed with the politician that far that they won't report that kind of information, what else is it that they're not reporting? What else is it that they don't see? I'm not putting bad motives on them. It is just that you tend not to see things that you should see when you get too close.[22]

Britton is far from the only editor who has been scooped on a story about a local politician by an out-of-town competitor. In 1992, shortly after Bob Packwood's election to a fifth term in the Senate, the *Washington Post* ran a story in which numerous women detailed allegations of sexual misconduct by the Oregon Republican.[23] Bumper stickers later mocked the slogan of the state's largest-circulation newspaper, the *Portland Oregonian*, for not breaking the story to Packwood's constituents first: "If it matters to Oregonians, it's in the *Washington Post*."

Stories that do not meet the editorial standards of local news editors sometimes find space in national outlets, after which they become fair game locally. Some stories are not even up to the news standards of the New York City tabloids, unless they first appear in another publication. The coverage of rumors about an extramarital affair between Mayor Rudy Giuliani and his communications director was one such story. In 1997, during the mayor's reelection campaign, articles in the *Los Angeles Times* and *Vanity Fair* magazine took the New York press to task for not reporting on the widespread rumors about the alleged difficulties in the Giuliani marriage. The city's highly competitive newspapers had only hinted about the story in gossip items and in articles about the mayor's wife's diminishing public role in his campaign. Local newspaper editors denied *Vanity Fair*'s assertion that they or their publishers spiked big stories about the suspected romance between the mayor and his aide because of personal, professional and political ties to the Giulianis.[24] As *New York Daily News* managing editor Arthur Browne put it at the time, the issue with the rumors was veracity, not cozy relationships between his newspaper and City Hall.

Browne said in an interview with the *Boston Globe* that he did not run the Giuliani rumors because his reporters could not prove that they were true. "This newspaper was probably the most aggressive organization in the city in pursuing the rumors. This included talking to dozens of people, watching people's living habits." So why run news stories about the *Vanity Fair* article, the *Globe* asked Browne, if the *News* itself could not prove the rumors were true—and the newspaper's own reporting raised doubts about the credibility of the magazine's account? "You face the issue: Is the presence of this, in a reputable national magazine that is vouching for its authority and accuracy—is the presence of this material in that magazine a newsworthy event in itself? Our judgment was, yes."[25] Other New York news organizations that had investigated the rumors about the mayor and his spokeswoman justified their subsequent coverage of the *Vanity Fair* allegations based on the public, on-the-record denials of Giuliani and his staff.

Editors in South Carolina faced a similar quandary a year later. *Time* magazine published a story in September 1998 that said South Carolina Democrats planned to use a scheduled deposition in a Freedom of Information Act lawsuit as an excuse to ask Republican governor David Beasley about whether he had an extramarital relationship with his former communications director. Extensive reporting prior to the *Time* story by the *State* newspaper in Columbia and other local news organizations produced no substantiation of the previously published rumors, which had circulated in South Carolina since at least 1996. This time, the governor confronted the gossip head-on. He, his wife, his former aide and her husband met reporters to deny an affair and blast the rumor-mongering. The joint news conference ended with a group hug. Beasley also sent a letter to the editor denying the "scurrilous lies" in *Time*.[26]

In Georgia that same year, state political reporters were likewise "big footed" by *George* magazine, which landed the first interview with gubernatorial candidate Mike Bowers's former mistress. The six-page story about the Republican candidate's fifteen-year extramarital relationship with his former secretary included a previously unreported detail: that Bowers was still sending his former lover a biweekly check to help her pay her bills. The former state attorney general met with reporters to say that his wife knew about and supported the payments to his ex-mistress. Later, as the controversy continued, he said he was ending them.[27]

No news organization can avoid being scooped, as reporters in Georgia and South Carolina were. Some sources will prefer opening up to a reporter from a famous national media outlet, whether for ego reasons or because an out-of-town journalist or a national magazine writer might have a different slant on a story than members of the local press. Decision-makers in state and local newsrooms can only control what they decide to write and broadcast. But increasingly those top editors and producers will need to consider another issue, especially when it comes to reporting on the private lives of political figures: What will they write when another news organization far away breaks a story on their beat, especially one they missed or already rejected? For now, those editorial decisions are apparently being made for them.

Internet

Online publishing gives nontraditional media such as alternative newspapers, and even entrepreneurial individuals, the national reach of many of the out-of-market news sources described above. This exciting and revolutionary development in media and communications also compounds many of the threats to political privacy posed by other alternative media.

President Clinton's secret "love child" with an Arkansas prostitute was not born on the Internet, but he grew up there. The story began offline with a February 1992 report in the *Globe* supermarket tabloid, which interviewed Bobbie Ann Williams about her claims of paid sexual encounters with then-Governor Clinton and her belief that her son, Danny, was the child of the Democratic presidential candidate. The mainstream press largely ignored the rumors about Clinton's illegitimate child, which political enemies began circulating in 1988. But the *Globe*'s story was similar to a plotline in *Primary Colors*, a fictionalized account of Clinton's first presidential campaign written by journalist Joel Klein after the 1992 election. The story of Danny Williams resurfaced along with numerous other rumors about Clinton's past during the Monica Lewinsky investigation six years later. In November 1998, in the heat of the House impeachment process, the Newsmax.com Web site interviewed the thirteen-year-old child's aunt about her family's desire to subject the president to a paternity test. Another online publication, the *Drudge Report*, announced in late December that DNA evidence in the Starr report to Congress gave the *Star* supermarket tabloid enough information to perform a blood test on Williams's son. White House press secretary Joe Lockhart was asked to respond during his daily news briefing, at which one reporter suggested that a photo of Danny Williams published on the Internet resembled Clinton. "That's good," the press secretary shot back. "And I'm an alien space baby." As in 1992, most news organizations ignored the story. The *New York Post* was one exception, reporting about the paternity test on its front page ("Clinton Paternity Bombshell"). The *Washington Times*, under a front-page banner headline, reported that most news organizations, including the *Times*, were not reporting on the rumors about an illegitimate presidential heir, which the *Times* then detailed. Despite the restraint of most of the press, millions of Americans learned about the paternity allegation anyway—and from an even more unconventional news source than Newsmax.com and the *Drudge Report*. On NBC's *Tonight Show*, host Jay Leno spent most of a week joking about the test. The story and the jokes largely ended when a report on the *Time* magazine Web site said the test result was negative. News wire reports and newscasts repeated the negative result across the country. But rumors about Clinton die hard on the Internet, especially on Web sites such as Newsmax.com, a conservative "news portal" based in Florida whose board of directors includes UPI president Arnaud de Borchgrave, former editor of the *Washington Times*. Bolstered by the conservative Accuracy in Media watchdog group, Newsmax.com questioned the validity of the DNA evidence presented in the Starr report, on which the *Star* tabloid based its paternity test.

It was easy for the press to dismiss the preposterous suggestion that independent counsel Kenneth Starr had somehow, even unintentionally, sought to exonerate the president by conspiring with the same tabloid that first reported Gennifer Flower's claims of an affair with then-candidate Clinton. However, reports on a number of other stories about Clinton did appear online first, often on the gossip page published by Matt Drudge, the Internet's self-styled Walter Winchell, whose editorial background consisted of a stint as store manager at a CBS gift shop. Before he broke the Monica Lewinsky story in January 1998, Drudge scooped *Newsweek* on its own story about Kathleen Willey, a former White House volunteer who had alleged that President Clinton made an unwanted sexual advance during an Oval Office conversation in 1993. In 1999, Drudge was first to report that NBC News was sitting on an on-the-record interview with Juanita Broaddrick, an Arkansas nursing home operator who said Clinton sexually assaulted her in a hotel room in 1978.

President Clinton is not the only target of online muckrakers. *Salon* magazine, an online magazine published in San Francisco, first reported in September 1998 that House Judiciary Committee chairman Henry Hyde participated in an extramarital affair with a married woman in the 1960s. Later, *Salon* published a lengthy article about U.S. Representative Dan Burton detailing numerous allegations of womanizing during his legislative and congressional career. Both *Salon* stories, especially Hyde's admission, were the subject of extensive follow-up reporting by traditional news organizations, including some whose reporters previously decided not to pursue the same tip on the Hyde story that led *Salon* to its scoop.

Some online publications, such as *Salon*, have staffs with traditional editorial backgrounds. Others, like the *Drudge Report*, are lone-wolf operations. Like alternative newspapers, online publications rarely have the same level of experienced editing that most traditional newsrooms have. And yet the Internet gives these new news sources potential distribution channels that rival many national and international media organizations. While online publications do not practice journalism the same way traditional newsrooms do, Internet sites such as *Drudge* and *Salon* exercise increasing influence over mainstream media decision-makers, if only by increasing the pressure to publish certain stories. To *Washington Post* columnist James K. Glassman, this competitive development is not entirely unhealthy:

> E-Journalism demands judgment not just from writers but from readers. Better yet, it reminds us that all journalism demands such judgment. We may feel better about a story because it has a brand name like AP or CBS attached, but skepticism is always warranted.[28]

Teaching readers how to be their own discerning cyber-sleuths is no easy task, since traditional news reporting based on Internet gossip sheets suggests that mainstream journalists have not learned that lesson themselves. Reminding readers why they cannot believe everything they read and hear, online and off, is perhaps journalism's most important mission in the online age. Or perhaps readers and television viewers are already better at making such judgments than those who cover the news are.

3

Unindicted
Coconspirators

The press takes most of the blame for the increasing scrutiny of political lives. But the rituals and practices of modern politics contribute greatly to the atmosphere that gives life to these stories. The role candidates and their campaigns play goes beyond nostalgic notions that elections are somehow nastier now than in the past. Politics has always been an ugly business in which the fear of personal embarrassment is a powerful weapon. While the press of years past was far more reluctant to report the personal indiscretions of politicians, such information was well known and considered fair game in the vetting of candidates. But this role was once performed behind closed doors by political parties, not by reporters, editors and producers.

While the press essentially ignored John F. Kennedy's extraordinary womanizing before and during his presidency, candidate Kennedy certainly expected his philandering to be an issue in his 1960 bid for the White House. Kennedy's extensive affairs were not widely reported until more than a decade after his assassination, when a congressional investigation detailed some of his activities. That might seem unbelievable in the era of Bill Clinton, whose own Kennedyesque romantic entanglements have made news since his first campaign for the White House in 1992. But differences in the Kennedy era and the Clinton era reflect changes in the way campaigns are waged as well as changes in media standards.

The generation of candidates who followed Kennedy into the television age of politics learned many tricks of the trade from popular entertainers, encouraging a degree of tabloid celebrity-watching previously reserved for movie and TV stars, athletes, and musicians. The emergence of "family values" as an issue has made a candidate's family life an issue, making aspiring officeholders vulnerable to accusations of hypocrisy. At the same time, new technologies available to the press are also available to inquisitive political rivals and enemies. Those investigative tools are giving rise to a new class of campaign operative— the opposition researcher. Recognizing these threats to their survival, candidates sometimes beat their opponents to the punch, revealing their own secrets to the press and their constituents. They may lose their privacy, but at least they gain some control over the political fallout.

CELEBRITY POLITICS

The transformation of the American politician from aspiring statesman to celebrity wannabe is a fairly recent development. The change is tied directly to the television camera's power to instantly reveal a candidate's or officeholder's personality in dimensions and details that were once found only in published letters and memoirs. The television camera required candidates to learn a new visual vocabulary—in speaking style, gesture, and appearance. Richard M. Nixon was among the first to exploit TV's power, with the deeply personal 1952 "Checkers" speech that salvaged his vice presidential candidacy. And he was among the medium's first victims—losing the presidency to a far more "telegenic" Democratic opponent in 1960. Although the evidence is inconclusive, it is widely believed that Nixon's shifty television persona in three nationally broadcast debates contributed to his narrow defeat. This perception decisively influenced the thinking and tactics of later politicians and their "handlers."

Nixon's less-analyzed role was as a trailblazer in using TV entertainment programs as a platform to stump for the White House. Starting with his 1960 bid, Nixon made several appearances on Jack Paar's late-night TV show, even playing the piano. During his successful 1968 campaign, Nixon memorably appeared on the popular *Laugh-In* comedy show, uncertainly misinflecting the program's trademark line, "Sock it to me."[1]

Nixon's TV appearances helped offset the former vice president's image as the dour loser of the 1960 presidential race and the California governor's race in 1962. They also established a new way to run for president. In June 1992, President Clinton appeared on *The Arsenio Hall Show* playing "Heartbreak Hotel" on his saxophone. Al Gore, Clinton's stilted vice president, tried to rework his own image with an appearance on David Letterman's show in 1993. Following in Nixon's footsteps by appropriating a comedian's signature catchphrase, Gore came armed with his own self-deprecating "Top Ten" list. (Item three in Gore's list of good things about being vice president: "You get to eat all the french fries the president can't get to."[2] During his aborted bid for president, former vice president Dan Quayle, the butt of more than his fair share of political potshots in late-night TV monologues, gamely visited NBC's Jay Leno on the air, as did Republican rival Elizabeth Dole, Democrat Bill Bradley and other White House contenders.

Such appearances are seemingly harmless. Handlers see these media events as inexpensive ways to reach broad audiences and, more importantly, to humanize their candidates. They are also opportunities to try to redefine a candidate's persona—to make the humorless seem funny, the lifeless look animated, and the foolish sound coherent. And, in many ways, appearing on entertainment TV programming is little different from such time-honored political activities as marching in a parade, shaking hands at a Nascar race, or throwing out the first ball at a base-ball game.

But by campaigning on popular television, candidates encourage their constituents to equate their appearances with the celebrities who regularly appear on these programs to plug CDs, movies and TV shows. At its worst, this practice can cheapen political discourse, reinforcing voters' fears that electoral contests are more about personality and popularity than substance. Moreover, by equating themselves with the pop-culture figures who are regularly dissected in supermarket tabloids and fanzines, candidates become vulnerable to similar types of scrutiny. At the same time, popular TV appearances contribute to the public's growing tendency to substitute entertainment venues for more substantive sources of political information. In a survey for the Pew Center for the People and the Press during the 1996 campaign, 25 percent of respondents said they sometimes or regularly learned about the presidential candidates from late-night TV comedy shows such as David Letterman's and Jay Leno's.[3]

Candidates who wish to be taken seriously should behave like serious people. Those who seek to "humanize" themselves in trivial ways turn themselves into human-interest stories, and will be treated as such by the press.

FAMILY VALUES AND HYPOCRISY

In this age of moral inexactitude and situational ethics it is easy to understand why candidates choose to emphasize "family values," that is, the collection of images and policies that conservative groups see as underpinning the traditional America family.

It is less easy to understand why candidates with messy personal lives choose to emphasize family values. Former Mississippi governor Kirk Fordice provides a particularly sad and extremely public example of one who did. Fordice ran for office as a candidate closely associated with the Christian right, projecting the image of a family man and loyal husband while making national headlines by pronouncing that the United States was a "Christian nation." At the same time, the governor secretly renewed his romance with a high school sweetheart.

Fordice might have kept this out of the news during his two terms in office except for three things. First was his 1993 surprise announcement that he and his wife planned to divorce. The announcement was not just news to the state but to Fordice's wife, who issued her own public statement contradicting the governor on their plans to separate. The couple then issued a joint press release saying they were working to salvage their marriage. Second was the governor's near-fatal car accident in 1996, when he overturned his Jeep returning to Jackson from a private lunch date with his girlfriend in Tennessee. News reports at the time said Fordice was seen with a woman other than his wife in a restaurant, holding hands and drinking wine before the accident, although police said alcohol was not a factor in the car wreck. Third was the governor's June 1999 vacation in France with his recently widowed girlfriend, who was photographed for the first time with Fordice by a television reporter as the couple exited a plane together during the return leg of their trip.

Shortly after Fordice's overseas trip with the woman, the governor once again announced plans to divorce. The "love gov," as a *New York Post* headline dubbed him, was perplexed by all the news coverage of his marriage, which ran on television and in newspapers across the country. "I'm trying to get a divorce from my wife and marry a sixty-five-year-old woman," he said in an interview with the *Delta Democrat Times*. "If that's a hot scoop in the press, God help us. Have we got anything to write about in Mississippi?"[4]

Hypocrisy is by no means the exclusive domain of conservative politicians. President Clinton, for instance, closely aligned himself with women's issues to maintain consistently high approval ratings among women throughout much of his presidency. However, Clinton's reckless philandering also put some of his most ardent political supporters in the women's movement in a difficult position, especially as the allegations against him increasingly resembled those against other politicians whose treatment of women earned condemnation. Hypocrisy can also extend into other areas of a politician's life and behavior, such as a tough-on-crime candidate who is caught breaking the law.

The American public is tolerant of many foibles, even from politicians, so long as they are not preceded by sanctimony and hypocrisy. Hypocrisy of any kind invites media scrutiny, often superseding informal statutes of limitation editors might accept on past behavior, such as an affair or a youthful brush with the law. But far worse, political hypocrisy can undermine the causes a politician holds most dear and increase public cynicism. It also opens lines of attack to one's political enemies.

TECHNOLOGY, "OPPO" AND ATTACKS

The same new technologies that are changing the way the press covers politics are also changing the way politicians practice their trade. These include both free and proprietary online databases that make it easier than ever to scour a politician's voting record and public statements for damaging material. Such databases include the THOMAS Web site maintained by the Library of Congress and the *Congressional Quarterly* "On

Congress" subscription Internet service. Services such as LEXIS-NEXIS also provide easy access to a researcher looking for state and local news coverage of a candidate at various stages of his or her career. An increasing number of legal filings are also recorded in online databases, as are a growing number of political transactions, such as campaign contributions.

These resources are essential tools for modern newsrooms, as detailed in chapter 2. But journalists do not have exclusive access to this kind of material. Candidates and their political consultants, especially a new breed of "opposition researchers," make extensive use of these information troves to quickly develop comprehensive data profiles of opponents. As the costs of building and accessing these databases drop, this style of cyber-sleuthing is increasingly available to candidates for state and even local office.

As matters of public record, there is nothing objectionable about the mining and use of such information. But information can be used to obfuscate and blur as much as it can bring enlightenment to public debate. And some information, no matter how it is uncovered, is unfair to use. Old-fashioned investigative techniques, including the use of hired private investigators, are not new in politics. Legal filings, including the court-sanctioned abuse of Freedom of Information Act requests, can become vehicles for prying into private matters. The continued use of these tactics by campaigns practically guarantees that certain kinds of disreputable information will work their way into campaigns.

For example, Colorado governor Roy Romer's longtime relationship with a female aide was revealed by *Insight* magazine in 1998, after many years of denials by all parties concerned. But the hard evidence on which the *Insight* story was based—images of Romer and his former aide engaged in an extended kiss in an airport parking lot—came from a team of private investigators hired by unnamed political enemies of the governor. Ironically, one of the private investigators involved in the surveillance of Romer told Denver newspapers that he had previously done work for the governor, trying to determine whether reporters from an alternative newspaper were tailing Romer to try to prove his affair.

Mark Taylor, the successful 1998 candidate for lieutenant governor in Georgia, was the target of a similar smear. In his case, the information came from sealed court records concerning a divorce case. Divorce and custody cases often provide nasty personal details for political operatives to mine. Often the information in such records is untrue or exaggerated. This is a common practice in divorce cases, in which lawyers use the threat of an embarrassing courtroom admission made under oath to seek a more favorable settlement for a client. Other times embarrassing information from such cases is true, as with Taylor's admitted marijuana and cocaine use. The way such information comes into play rarely gets the news coverage it deserves. In this case, it should have been as big a story as Taylor's admitted offense. Taylor's admission of illegal drug use in a sealed deposition was sent anonymously to reporters at the *Macon Telegraph*, which based a news story on the material after Taylor confirmed the details of his deposition. The source of the material was never reported. Although Taylor went on to win the race, the admission of drug use was the subject of attacks by his opponents in both the Democratic primary and the general election campaign. Taylor's GOP opponent even ran television ads suggesting Taylor had an ongoing drug problem without offering any evidence to substantiate the allegation.

South Carolina governor David Beasley was the target of a more up-front attack by his opponents. Late in the governor's unsuccessful campaign for a second term, lawyers for the state Democratic Party told *Time* magazine that they planned to use a scheduled deposition in an upcoming Freedom of Information lawsuit as an opportunity to ask the married governor under oath about a long-rumored romance with a top aide. The rumor was not new; it had circulated in state political circles for more than two years. The deposition was canceled, but the legal ploy succeeded in generating news coverage of the damaging and completely unsubstantiated allegations across the state.

As devastatingly effective as these tactics can be in some political races, such attacks are not always prudent. Gutter tactics of this sort almost guarantee retribution and retaliation, even if they do not immediately backfire, as they did against Taylor's opponents in Georgia. They also sour voters, political activists, and possible candidates, regardless of party affiliation. Like industrial pollution that enriches a company but poisons the atmosphere, such tactics poison the political process, depress voter turnout and discourage involvement. Even when these forces can be harnessed for political gain, their long-term effects will ultimately scar—if not tar—almost anyone involved in campaigns and elections at any level.

PREEMPTIVE DISCLOSURE

The most effective way to defuse a political time bomb ticking in a candidate's closet is full disclosure. Revealing secrets allows a politician to choose the time and place of the disclosure. By negotiating with a media outlet for an exclusive story, a public confession may offer increased control over the terms of the disclosure. However, disclosure does not guarantee a politician safe passage through scandal. Of course, it is far easier to offer this advice than to take it. Apart from the guests on *The Jerry*

Springer Show, most people find it humiliating to reveal their most embarrassing foibles to friends, neighbors, and supporters.

Republican Robert Livingston, the Louisiana congressman chosen to succeed Newt Gingrich as Speaker of the House after the 1998 elections, demonstrated the downside of public disclosure in December 1998. Days before the House vote to impeach President Clinton, Livingston stunned his colleagues with the admission that he had occasionally "strayed" from his marriage. Livingston's revelation was prompted by pornographer Larry Flynt's anti-impeachment–motivated investigation of various congressmen's personal lives. While most of Livingston's colleagues expressed their support for him despite his admission, some conservative congressmen grumbled behind the scenes about their newly selected leader's past. Not wanting to compromise the slim Republican voting majority, Livingston stepped aside and, in a speech during the House impeachment debate, announced his decision to retire.

Livingston's public confession and his decision to relinquish the speakership did have some benefits for his family. His wife successfully lobbied Flynt and Louisiana media outlets to not pursue additional information on her husband's dalliances, based on the price he'd already paid, his imminent departure from public life and her forgiveness. Livingston also satisfied reporters' only legitimate and lingering question by publicly denying that any of his affairs involved women with whom he had a professional relationship.[5]

Successfully inoculating oneself against a truthful political allegation requires a complete confession. Reporters are trained to sniff out inconsistency. A public admission of wrongdoing will only pass this "sniff test" if one picks a story and sticks with it. It helps, of course, if the story is true, as painful as the truth may be.

Consider the case of Republican congressman Dan Burton. His 1998 confession that he fathered a child out of wedlock was intended to preempt an expected exposé by *Vanity Fair*. A freelance writer under contract with the magazine was probing rumors about Burton's past sex life, especially during his term in the state senate. At a constituent forum in his Indiana district, Burton prepared voters for the expected news about his past with a warning to expect to read something scandalous about him. A short time later, Burton publicly revealed his secret. *Vanity Fair* then canceled its profile, but the writer shopped the story to a number of other news organizations, including CBS's *60 Minutes*. Eventually, the online magazine *Salon* published the story, which included numerous unsubstantiated allegations of infidelity. While some charges were better documented than others, most news organizations gave the *Salon* report little attention. The *Washington Post*, for example, produced a front-page story about unusual financial arrangements involving a female staffer paid by the congressman's official and campaign offices. However, the *Post* did not focus on implications of a personal relationship between the woman and the congressman.[6]

Beyond the potential for pain that the revelation strategy holds for those who adopt it, a downside for other public officials is the precedent that it sets. Each time a politician steps before the cameras and microphones to reveal his or her sins, it sets a new standard for disclosure, validates a new line of questioning and heralds a new wave of potential scandal.

4

Out of Order

Among the many journalistic offenses detailed in this volume, one pattern of press behavior stands out: the obsessive focus on personal foibles that distorts traditional news standards, especially during a political scandal. Smears and gossip that are usually the topic of off-the-record banter suddenly appear in print and on the air. Old rumors are dusted off and reexamined, and allegations of misconduct are resurrected, even if they've already been addressed publicly. Everything a politician now says and everything he or she has ever done are viewed through the distorting prism of the controversy at hand.

Numerous forces contribute to this self-destructive media process. They include professional adrenaline, deadline pressure, peer pressure, accelerated news cycles, a fear of being scooped, and a desire to move the story forward, to name several. Collectively they produce reporting that violates journalists' own sensibilities, distorts the political process, and diminishes public confidence in the fourth estate. Several manifestations of this press behavior deserve special scrutiny: out-of-context references to a political figure's personal conduct, the mining of politicians' pasts for questionable behavior of dubious relevance to his or her public responsibilities, and the increasingly frequent publication and broadcast of unsourced and unsubstantiated political rumors.

OUT OF CONTEXT

Revelations about a politician's personal life, even those that are unquestionably newsworthy, can unfairly dominate his or her overall coverage. For example, news stories in Georgia newspapers about 1998 gubernatorial candidate Mike Bowers dwelled endlessly on the impact of his admitted extramarital affair. At times this gave the coverage a catch-22 quality; even when the issue did not come up on the campaign trail, its absence was treated as newsworthy. Thus, under the headline, "Bowers' affair not a topic at GOP breakfast," the *Atlanta Journal and Constitution* reported that the candidate "was not asked a single question about the affair" by seventy Republicans attending a party event in Sewanee, Georgia. When Bowers tried to make an issue of a competitor's wealth by releasing his personal tax returns and challenging his Republican rivals to do the same, the Atlanta newspapers put that story as well in the context of Bowers's sex life. "By releasing his own returns, Bowers hoped to focus attention on issues other than the personal controversy over his longtime extramarital affair," the *Journal and Constitution* reported in the fourth paragraph of its story about the tax returns. No statements quoted in the story, even from Bowers's competitors, supported the newspapers' prominent claim. The story noted as well that an upcoming issue of *George* magazine would also revisit the romance.[1]

Putting campaign events in context for voters is a legitimate function of journalism. But reporters should not make an issue out of a topic that is clearly not relevant to the story at hand. It is the gratuitous references to a personal scandal that outrage ordinary readers and viewers as well as public officials. In 1998, for example, Congressman Dan Burton refused to answer questions in a candidate questionnaire from the *Indianapolis Star* because he was unhappy with the newspaper's coverage of his sex life. In each of four weekly installments, the *Star* repeated the following statement in the place it had reserved for the congressman's answers to questions on taxes, the budget surplus, health care, school vouchers, campaign finance, and, of course, public morality:

> Burton, through his spokesman John Williams, said he had "absolutely nothing to say to anyone at the *Star and News*, given last month's coverage." He was referring to articles about his admission that he fathered a child out of wedlock.[2]

By printing this statement, the *Star* appeared to be trying to embarrass Burton into participating in its conversation with the candidates. However, repeating the statement week after week made the *Star* seem petty and vindictive. (In any case, neither Burton's refusal to respond to the newspaper's questionnaire nor its coverage of his past sex life affected the outcome of that year's election. The congressman's strongly Republican district reelected Burton with more than 70 percent of the vote.)

OLD NEWS

Some stories about political figure are like zombies—old news reanimated from newspaper clipping files and electronic morgues. Others are like mummies—long-forgotten or long-hidden episodes unearthed and put on display many years later. Both kinds of stories can be monstrously unfair. As noted earlier, Arizona senator John McCain exorcised his demons by discussing his past "dalliances" in interviews with journalist Robert Timberg for the 1995 book *The Nightingale's Song*. Timberg's book documents the impact of Vietnam on the lives on several prominent Naval Academy graduates who served in the war. In one passage, paraphrased in numerous interviews and early campaign profiles of the Republican presidential candidate, Timberg describes the failure of McCain's first marriage in 1980 and the womanizing that preceded it, after McCain returned from a Vietnamese prison camp and took up a post in Jacksonville, Florida, in 1974:

> Off-duty, usually on routine cross-country flights to Yuma and El Centro, John started carousing and running around with women. To make matters worse, some of the women with whom he was linked by rumor were his subordinates. In some ways, the rumors were an extension of the John McCain stories that had swirled in his wake since Academy days—some true, some with an element of truth, others patently absurd. Asked about them, he admitted to having a series of dalliances during this period, but flatly denied any with females, officer or enlisted, under his command.[3]

Timberg also spoke to McCain's first wife, Carol, about the breakup, which she said had less to do with the war and her disfiguring car accident while he was a prisoner of war in Vietnam than it did with other factors. "I attribute it more to John turning forty and wanting to be twenty-five again than I do to anything else," she said.[4]

Timberg's account of the McCain breakup, with all its embarrassing revelations, should have been more than enough detail for any reporter profiling the senator. But the conventions of journalism do not work that way. Each reporter feels personally obliged to ask the tough question, even if the subject refuses to discuss the matter any further. During the first months of McCain's White House bid, interviewers from CNN, CBS, ABC, and other media outlets all asked for more details about McCain's divorce and womanizing, which the candidate rightly refused to provide. On ABC's *20/20*, Sam Donaldson asked McCain to comment on "widely written" accounts that "when you got back from prison, you resumed the womanizing habits you had as a young man." On CBS's *60 Minutes*, Mike Wallace phrased the adultery question as a statement: "After Vietnam, you come back, you're married. You begin to carouse again. You're not the most faithful of husbands. So your marriage to Carol unravels." On CBS's *Sunday Morning*, Rita Braver added a new angle to the question: "You admitted to infidelity in your first marriage. Are you worried about the scrutiny that you and your family will have to undergo in this campaign?" McCain's answer to each question was roughly the same: He took responsibility for the divorce and refused to discuss the matter in any greater detail.[5]

The relevance of past affairs is hard to judge. News organizations probably would not have revealed Henry Hyde's extramarital relationship in the 1960s if the Illinois Republican had not been presiding over the House Judiciary Committee's 1998 hearings on articles of impeachment against President Clinton. *Salon*, a three-year-old online magazine, broke the Hyde story in September 1998, arguing in an accompanying editorial that the independent counsel and congressional probes of Clinton justified its reporting on the chairman's affair:

> In a different and better world, we would not have released this story. Throughout the tragic farce of the Clinton-Lewinsky scandal, we have strongly argued that the private lives of all

Americans, whether they are public figures or not, should remain sacrosanct. . . .

But Clinton's enemies have changed the rules. In the brave new world that has been created by the Clinton-Lewinsky scandal, the private lives of public figures are no longer off-limits. . . .

Aren't we fighting fire with fire, descending to the gutter tactics of those we deplore? Frankly, yes. But ugly times call for ugly tactics. When a pack of sanctimonious thugs beats you and your country upside the head with a tire-iron, you can withdraw to the sideline and meditate, or you can grab it out of their hands and fight back.[6]

Salon's decision that the nearly thirty-year-old affair was newsworthy depended on the magazine's belief that the Lewinsky story was really just about sex and that the coverage of it made the sex lives of all public officials fair game. "This opens a Pandora's box, and Ken Starr and the Republicans opened that box up," *Salon* editor David Talbot, who wrote the Hyde story, said on ABC's *Good Morning America* the day after the article was published.[7] However, critical differences distinguish Hyde's affair and President Clinton's behavior. The president was accused of lying under oath about his sexual relationship with Monica Lewinsky; Hyde was not. In addition, Hyde's twenty-nine-year-old paramour was a hair stylist in no way connected to the forty-one-year-old lawyer's professional responsibilities. In fact, the four-year relationship began the year before Hyde was first elected to the Illinois state house in 1966.

Most important, as Hyde said in his statement to *Salon*, the story was just old news. "The statute of limitations has long since passed on my youthful indiscretions," Hyde said.[8] Hyde's definition of "youthful indiscretion" was clearly a stretch, even for a man of seventy-four. Nevertheless, the fact that his marriage endured another twenty-three years, until his wife's death in 1992, should be a factor in gauging the news value of Hyde's long-ago affair in relation to his present-day responsibilities.

The decision to publish the Hyde story was controversial even within *Salon*. The online magazine's Washington bureau chief, Jonathan Broder, was forced to resign after he spoke on the record to the *Washington Post* about his journalistic objections.[9] Other news organizations were also aware of Hyde's affair but ignored the same tip that sparked *Salon*'s investigation. The source of *Salon*'s reporting was Norm Sommer, a seventy-two-year-old Florida retiree. He had spent most of 1998 trying to convince numerous news organizations (among them, the *Los Angeles Times*, the *Chicago Tribune*, the *Boston Globe*, and the *Miami Herald*) to pursue the matter. "I tried to get the story out for seven and a half months," Sommer told *Salon*. "I've spent hundreds of hours and called dozens of people in the media, without success."[10]

The initial restraint of the news organizations that Sommer contacted is a reminder that most mainstream media managers and reporters do not necessarily bite at every scandal tidbit that is offered. But a decision by any news organization, for whatever reason and based on whatever standards it applies, can provoke a public reaction that forces other editors to practice least-common-denominator journalism, in which they end up publishing or broadcasting stories they might otherwise ignore. Once Hyde spoke publicly about his affair, and his GOP colleagues called for FBI investigations of whether the White House was *Salon*'s actual source, traditional news organizations had little choice but to follow up.

RUMORS

Political lore holds that Gary Hart lit the match that set his presidential candidacy ablaze in 1987 by challenging reporters to stake him out to test gossip about his womanizing. "Follow me around," Hart had said. "If anyone wants to put a tail on me, go ahead." In reality, though, the *Miami Herald* published its story revealing Hart's relationship with a Florida model on the same day the *New York Times* first published Hart's famous challenge to reporter E. J. Dionne Jr. Hart's reckless personal behavior suggests that his campaign for the White House may well have self-destructed on its own, if not at the hands of a rival. In a 1990 interview with two of the authors, then–Republican Party chairman Lee Atwater denied rumors that he had somehow masterminded the Donna Rice incident to help the candidacy of then–vice president George Bush. "I wasn't behind it," Atwater said, "but if I had been, I would have waited until the son of a bitch got the nomination and I'd have broken it then!"

Hart was as much the victim of unfair media rumor-mongering as he was of his own weaknesses. Ironically, the tip that led to Hart's downfall was not just a byproduct of mediacirculated rumors, but a press account denouncing media-circulated rumors. As he was setting out on his second bid for the Democratic presidential nomination, news reports often mentioned his suspected womanizing. Some stories described supporters and fund-raisers as being nervous about the gossip. Other articles suggested that Hart's opponents were quietly spreading stories about the front-runner. When Tom Fiedler, then politics editor of the *Miami Herald*, wrote a column denouncing the media scandal-mongering, a reader called to comment—and to offer a tip. The caller's friend, Donna Rice, was involved with Hart and headed to Washington from Florida for a weekend rendezvous. The *Herald*'s subsequent stakeout of

Hart and reporting about his weekend with Rice doomed Hart's candidacy.[11]

Although many news stories begin as gossip or rumor, printing or broadcasting unsubstantiated rumors tarnishes journalism's reputation. Published rumors also push a news story along unfairly—accelerating Hart's destruction, for instance. As in Hart's case, many political rumors turn out to be true. Other rumors reporters know—or at least suspect—are true, but the information is not sourced reliably enough to print or broadcast. With increasing frequency, however, unsubstantiated and destructive personal rumors are finding their way into American political journalism.

One such rumor, which ultimately proved true, was the existence of Monica Lewinsky's semen-stained blue dress. The dress provided DNA evidence proving Lewinsky's sexual relationship with President Clinton. The former White House aide turned the critical piece of evidence over to independent counsel Kenneth W. Starr after striking an immunity agreement in late July 1998. But unproven rumors about the dress's existence were widely reported—and even widely debunked—six months earlier, in the first weeks of the scandal, based on little evidence and the comments of one unnamed source.

By the time the mainstream press first reported the Lewinsky investigation on January 21, 1998, virtual gossip Matt Drudge was already writing about a possible "DNA trail" implicating the president on his online tip sheet, the *Drudge Report*. Drudge's unsourced item was based on comments Lewinsky supposedly made about a "garment" that she kept and "allegedly said she would never wash." The next day, Drudge spread the story to a mainstream news audience during interviews with Mary Matalin on her radio talk show and with NBC's Matt Lauer on *The Today Show*. Drudge said on *Today* that the information was based on information Lewinsky had shared in phone conversations secretly recorded by Linda Tripp, a friend and Pentagon coworker of Lewinsky's.

> Lauer: You say Monica Lewinsky has a piece of clothing that might have the president's semen on it?
>
> Drudge: She has bragged this to Mrs. Tripp, who has told this to investigators, it's my understanding. And currently the independent counsel's office is furious with me for letting this go.
>
> Lauer: But you don't have any confirmation of that?
>
> Drudge: Not outside what I've just heard, but I don't think anybody does at this point.[12]

NBC soiled its own reputation by giving Drudge an audience to discuss unconfirmed and unsubstantiated information that it would not report on its own. Lucianne Goldberg, a conservative New York literary agent and Clinton detractor who convinced Tripp to tape her phone calls with Lewinsky, later said publicly that she was Drudge's original source on the dress story. Additional reporting on the topic was based on better sources than Drudge's account, but not much. And stories based entirely on accounts by other news organizations (including secondhand media reports about what Drudge was reporting—even the usually dependable *New York Times*) perpetuated and spread erroneous information.

The night after Drudge's NBC appearance, ABC reported on the dress at the top of its evening newscast. Introducing the story, anchor Peter Jennings attributed the information to "someone with specific knowledge of what it is that Monica

Lewinsky says really took place between her and the president." Reporter Jackie Judd said, "According to the source, Lewinsky says she saved, apparently as a kind of souvenir, a navy blue dress with the president's semen stain on it. If true, this could provide some physical evidence of what really happened."[13]

Confusion about the dress began with a muddled report in the next day's *New York Times*, which mistook the rumored semen-stained dress with another garment that sources had said President Clinton gave to Lewinsky. The *Times* account was based on information from the Tripp tapes leaked by "investigators":

> Investigators who have heard the tapes said Ms. Lewinsky made references to gifts she had received from President Clinton, including a dress. On one of the tapes, the investigators said, Ms. Lewinsky tells a friend, Linda R. Tripp, that the dress contains a semen stain from President Clinton. It was not known whether the special prosecutor has subpoenaed the dress.[14]

The gift dress, as it turned out, was really a separate item of clothing—a long T-shirt Clinton bought for Lewinsky during a family vacation. Whether the *Times* or its sources confused the two items of clothing is not clear. When Lewinsky's lawyer said on television that weekend that he was not aware of any "dress that might be forensically important in terms of DNA evidence," as he delicately phrased it on ABC's *This Week*, doubts about the story began to creep into the reporting.[15] On January 27, the *Washington Post* reported that President Clinton told a friend, "There is no dress." The *Post* said, "It was not clear whether the president was referring to reports of a dress containing incriminating evidence or a dress he reportedly gave Lewinsky as a gift."[16]

More reporting over the following week added to the confusion. After a January 29 CBS News report that FBI tests found no evidence of semen stains on clothing seized from Lewinsky's apartment, reporters began to assume the story was untrue. *Time* magazine dissected the dress coverage in a story about the "anatomy of a salacious leak, and how it ricocheted around the walls of the media echo chamber." *Washington Post* media critic Howard Kurtz wrote about the sources for press coverage of "supposed evidence," including "the imaginary semen-stained dress."[17]

Five months later, when the "imaginary semen-stained dress" actually materialized, many journalists were stunned. Lewinsky had hidden the garment at her mother's New York apartment, where Starr's investigators overlooked it. In Grand Jury testimony on August 6, Lewinsky said that the dress "wasn't a souvenir," she just had not gotten around to cleaning it before the story about her relationship with the president broke. She also said that she wasn't sure the stain was President Clinton's semen, that it might have been "spinach dip," since she believed she wore the same dress to dinner that evening.[18]

In *Warp Speed: America in the Age of Mixed Media*, respected former journalists Bill Kovach and Tom Rosenstiel used coverage of the Lewinsky scandal to document how competition, especially from alternative news sources such as the Internet, is increasing competitive pressures to run poorly sourced news stories. One example Kovach and Rosenstiel examined in detail was the blue dress story. "Before a news organization goes with a story, it needs to consider whether it has sourcing that is thorough enough that the account will be understood and believed," Kovach and Rosenstiel concluded. "Making stories as clear and credible as possible, even if it means waiting, may also protect against stories being mischaracterized in subsequent versions as they echo through the media."[19] The errors and confusion in the rush to report the news about the blue dress proves the point that process matters in evaluating scandal coverage. While many of the early news reports about the possible existence of the dress turned out to be accurate, especially Jackie Judd's carefully worded January 23 news report on ABC, Judd and other journalists were in many ways lucky, given the sources on whom they depended for their information. Other news organizations that reported on the blue dress should find no vindication in the outcome of the Starr investigation. If the standard is that sloppy reporting is acceptable so long as poorly sourced rumors eventually turn out to be true, then Matt Drudge has replaced David Broder as dean of the Washington press corps.

There is even a growing attitude that circulating rumors is permissible because it is somehow antidemocratic for journalists to withhold information. "Even for traditional media journalists, furtive rumors of dalliance are enough—at least to gossip about among themselves, if not to share with their readers or viewers," wrote Michael Kinsley, editor of the Microsoft-owned online publication *Slate,* in a February 1998 essay for *Time* magazine. "There is something slightly elitist about the attitude that we journalists can be trusted to evaluate such rumors appropriately but that our readers and viewers cannot. Actually, though, almost everybody has the same standards— that is, almost none—in passing along juicy rumors to friends and colleagues."[20]

No such "elitism" hampered the early presidential campaign coverage of Texas governor George W. Bush. Rumors about the Republican candidate's partying in his college years and bachelor days were so widespread that many mainstream news organizations appeared to give little thought to repeating the latest gossip, regardless of the source. In March 1999, the supermarket tabloid the *Star* quoted an anonymous source who described a nude photograph of the Republican candidate "cavorting atop a bar in a drunken stupor" during a college party. Millions of Americans learned about the rumored photograph from Jay Leno's monologues on NBC's *Tonight Show*. ("These Republican spin doctors, they're working hard to discredit this story." Leno said one night. "They said today that even if George Bush Jr. were dancing naked on a bar, no one got stained."[21]) Two days earlier, a "Page Six" gossip item in the *New York Post* had summarized the *Star*'s story and its sourcing. But as the story quickly worked its way into more conventional journalistic outlets, its source and veracity became increasingly blurry.

The *Post*'s more reserved cross-town cousin, the *New York Times*, mentioned the tabloid report about the photo in a snide column about Bush's "frat boy" image by Pulitzer Prize–winning commentator Maureen Dowd. Asked to respond to the *Star*'s story, Bush spokeswoman Karen Hughes told Dowd, "Yeah, and green aliens have landed on the lawn of the governor's mansion." Dowd repeated the rumor again—this time without attribution —in a humorous June 1999 column, in which she wrote about the Republican Party's infatuation with Bush. Dowd said, "Republicans should remain besotted as long as their crush can pass a few simple tests," one of which was that "if a nude picture of W. dancing on a bar does show up, it will be flattering and have good lighting."[22]

Some news accounts about the rumors noted that the *Star*'s story had not "panned out," as Steve Chapman put it in the *Chicago Tribune*.[23] In a front-page story in May 1999, the *Wall Street Journal* detailed its unsuccessful efforts to track down the sources of various rumors about Bush—including the nude photo story.

The photo has been written about in the *Star* tabloid, and its existence has been hinted at on the Internet. The gossip is so prevalent that Dorothy Koch, the governor's sister, even raised the possibility with their mother, former first lady Barbara Bush, of releasing naked-baby pictures of her brother, Ms. Koch says. "We all think it's hilarious," says Ms. Koch.[24]

Bush himself discussed the alleged photograph in an interview for the June 1999 issue of *Texas Monthly* magazine, which included a multipart cover story on him. "I don't think there is one," Bush said of the picture. "I'm too modest to have danced on a bar naked."[25] Some news organizations repeated Bush's denial, but his statement did not make the rumor disappear. A profile of the governor in the *Washington Post* the following month also made reference to the photograph in the context of Bush's intentional strategy of inoculating himself against public backlash to press reports about his "irresponsible" youth. "Bush seems to realize that he has created something of a political monster through this approach, spawning countless rumors that have him doing everything from dancing naked on a bar to copping cocaine on a Washington street," the *Post* reported.[26] At the time of this writing, no source has produced a copy of the much-discussed photograph, and no credible source has provided any public evidence that it even exists. Nonetheless, this rumor has received a significant public airing.

Even when unsubstantiated, rumors can be serious news, as when Ronald Reagan joined a Republican whispering campaign by suggesting that 1988 Democratic presidential nominee Michael Dukakis had mental health problems, or when allies of House Speaker Jim Wright tried to delay his ouster in 1989 by smearing his possible successors. In both cases, however, the sources of the rumors and the veracity of the gossip were essential details, without which journalists would have been reporting unfair information out of context. Not repeating the source of a published or broadcast rumor clouds its significance and confuses readers and viewers, blurring the line between fact and innuendo. Salacious gossip repeated in print or on the air without sources or any effort to verify facts is not journalism. It is smut.

5

The Verdict

Colin L. Powell was preparing to step before more than three dozen television cameras and deliver the news that had already seeped out: The popular retired Army general and first black chairman of the Joint Chiefs of Staff would sit out the 1996 campaign for the White House. Polls showed that Powell was the only Republican likely to best incumbent Democrat Bill Clinton on Election Day a year hence. But as NBC anchorman Tom Brokaw broke into the day's programming to present Powell's news conference, he said one reason for the general's decision was well known. "It is widely believed that his wife, Alma, had a major role in this decision," Brokaw said. "She has a long history of depression, and that no doubt would get a very vigorous examination by not only the general's political opponents but also by reporters."[1]

In fact, the press had already explored the issue of Alma Powell's depression. Dick Polman and Steve Goldstein of the *Philadelphia Inquirer* first reported that she used medication to treat depression. The news was mentioned briefly in a long, front-page story about Powell's possible candidacy more than two weeks earlier. "A close family friend said the Powells consider her condition a minor situation but understand it has to be considered in a family decision of this magnitude," the *Inquirer* reported.[2] *Newsweek* magazine confirmed the report a week later, giving Alma Powell's depression and "worries about the family's privacy" slightly more play than the *Inquirer* in a long article about Powell's campaign contemplation and a sidebar about his wife's role.[3]

At Powell's news conference, however—after Brokaw had already cut away to analyze the ongoing event—the general contradicted the anchorman's introduction. Alma's depression was not a major factor in his decision to sit out the race, he said in answer to a reporter's question, "and we found no offense in what was written about it."

> My wife has depression. She's had it for many, many years, and we have told many, many people about it. It is not a family secret. It is very easily controlled with proper medication, just as my blood pressure is sometimes under control with proper medication.
>
> And you obviously don't want your whole family life out in the press, but when the story broke we confirmed it immediately, and I hope that people who read that story who think they might be suffering from depression make a bee-line to the doctor, because it is something that can be dealt with very easily.[4]

Increasing media scrutiny no doubt takes its toll on public figures and their families. The promise of higher pay in the private sector (without prying personal examinations by the press) is appealing. At the same time, the fear that intrusive reporters are driving "good people" out of politics is perhaps overstated, as it was in Colin Powell's case. Media scrutiny can also be a deterrent to scoundrels who might seek political office. In some ways, the consequences of intensive press focus on the private lives of politicians are as great on the press itself as they are on those in politics, at least as measured by public confidence in the credibility of reporters and reporters' confidence in themselves. But the focus of public debate about the issue of political privacy is almost always on the quality candidates who are driven from the process, and the mediocre political figures who are left behind.

Political commentary bemoaning significant numbers of congressional retirements in the 1990s contributed to the sense that the best political leaders are abandoning public service. In the three election cycles that ran from 1991 to 1996, twenty-nine members of the Senate retired, including a record thirteen members in 1996. That was more than the total number of Senate retirements in the previous six cycles. In the same three election cycles, 162 members of the House voluntarily relinquished their seats at the end of their terms. That included a record sixty-five House retirements in 1992, when a check-kiting scandal involving the House of Representatives bank endangered many incumbents' chances for reelection.

The situation was very different in 1998. Even in the midst of the Monica Lewinsky investigation and embarrassing revelations about the personal lives of several prominent Republican congressmen, just four senators and twenty-three members of the House gave up their seats. Both 1998 figures were well below the average number of congressional retirements since 1950. The dropoff in congressional departures suggests that the high number of retirements earlier in the 1990s might have had less to do with the burdens of service than with the political shifts that gave Republicans control of both chambers of Congress for the first time since 1955.[5]

Congressional retirements have indeed depleted the ranks of House and Senate moderates, making the legislative branch a less civil and more partisan place to work. That increasing partisanship also makes Congress a firetrap for political scandal and intrigue. The way the media frames political debate contributes, too, particularly in pyrotechnic talk television and radio formats that give prominence to those who most disagree on an issue. The redistricting process after the 1990 census was another factor. The creation of many minority districts meant that those running for other seats were campaigning in far less ideologically diverse areas. The isolation of certain voting blocs after 1990, particularly of ethnic voters, meant many candidates did not need to appeal to a broad range of voters to win their races.

Some fret that this political climate is only favorable to partisan, blow-dried, sound-biting politicians. But any long-term observer or member of Congress will tell you that the body's current membership is, in general, far better informed, better educated, and in many ways better at communicating than in the past. The vast majority are bright and able, and achieve a fair amount, whether or not one agrees with the object of the members' efforts. This is one subject on which serious reporters, academics, and politicians are agreed. Fifty years ago, many good people served in Congress who could not be elected in the television age. Being good on TV, however, does not mean being a bad public servant. To the contrary, it means one has the communication skills to build support for a public agenda. This can be critical in a country with a growing population that cares much less about politics than in the past.

People who lament the passing of the so-called golden age of public service either have poor memories or weren't alive at all. If law enforcement had been as tough and as thorough in investigating public officials fifty years ago as it is today, and if Congress itself had policed its members then to the extent that it does now, it would have been a good year when a dozen members were not indicted. The degree of corruption in politics is no higher now than in decades past. Reforms passed after Watergate, especially financial disclosure requirements, ensure that the degree of corruption may in fact be far less than it once was. The sins of the past are simply forgotten, because reporters frequently failed to report them and law enforcement failed to pursue them.

The same is true in presidential politics, despite an even more intense media spotlight on nearly every corner of a White House candidate's life. While Bill Clinton may be deficient in his personal morality, he is also one of the smartest and most knowledgeable individuals ever to sit in the Oval Office. And despite the scrutiny that will inevitably follow Clinton's tumultuous two terms, the initial crop of major party contenders who set out to run for the White House in 1999 included a two-term incumbent vice president, a former vice president, a former senator, two former Cabinet secretaries, a current governor, a House committee chairman, three current senators and two former White House advisers.

The field of prospective presidents in 2000 offers more experience and more diversity of views and is arguably a better crop of candidates than in 1960, when the field included three future presidents, one of whom was an incumbent vice president, and one future vice president—all of whom served in the Senate. Further, the presidential debates of the 1960 campaign did not include any discussion of the New Frontier, the Great Society, or the dramatic gestures of international peace and détente on which the three future presidents running that year would base their legacies. Nostalgia should not blind our assessment of past political campaigns, heroes and villains.

All of this is not to minimize the impact of attack journalism on the electoral process. While ambition has provided a healthy antidote to the poison pens of some reporters, the "politics of personal destruction" inevitably takes its toll. A democracy is based on electing human representatives with human failings. But some qualified candidates will remain on the sidelines rather than submit themselves and their families to a grueling personal examination by the press and their opponents. Even candidates standing on top of the polls have stood aside.

Moreover, the level of scrutiny once applied only to candidates for the highest offices is being applied farther down the ballot. In Georgia, for example, Lieutenant Governor Pierre Howard dropped out of the 1998 Democratic gubernatorial contest, relinquishing his front-runner status fifteen months before the election because of the impact on his family. Howard's announcement came two months after the leading Republican in the race, Mike Bowers, confessed to a long-standing extramarital affair that cost him critical support among his party's conservative wing. At the August 1997 news conference announcing his decision, Howard denied he was bowing out of the race to prevent any Bowers-like revelation about himself. "There is nothing in my background that worried me and caused me to want to get out of the race," Howard told suspicious reporters.[6] Almost two weeks later, Jim Wooten, editor of the *Atlanta Journal*'s editorial page, wrote that suspicions lingered nonetheless.

> People looking for some dark reason that he withdrew are likely to find it to be nothing more than he stated: His family was not into it. Neither was he.
>
> Since Howard's abrupt announcement, the state has been abuzz with speculation. The most plausible explanation, after 10 days of conversation with people in politics—an industry that ri-

vals journalism in its inability to keep a secret—
is that there are no secrets to keep.[7]

And that is the level of scrutiny applied to a *former* gubernatorial candidate.

The public and the press are deeply divided on the importance and the impact of this kind of reporting. A 1998–1999 survey conducted by the Pew Research Center for the People and the Press for the Committee for Concerned Journalists clearly showed this divide. The Pew Center surveyed 552 journalists, editors and news executives from both national and local media outlets and compared the numbers with the results of a national telephone survey of general public opinion. About half of those in the news survey—49 percent of national media and 56 percent of local outlets—said news organizations' coverage of the personal and ethical aspects of public figures is intended to drive controversy. In contrast, almost three-quarters of the public—72 percent—said news organizations are more interested in the controversy than in reporting the news on such stories. The division is more dramatic when asked about journalists' roles as public watchdogs. Almost 90 percent in the media said criticism by news organizations keeps political leaders from "doing things that should not be done." Only a small majority of the public, 55 percent, agrees—down from 67 percent in a 1985 poll. At the same time, a growing number said press criticism was keeping political leaders "from doing their jobs"— 39 percent in the 1998–1999 survey, up from 17 percent in the 1985 poll.[8]

Many journalists contend that their readers and viewers are hypocritical on these questions. They point to increased circulation and TV ratings of scandal news to make their case. After all, almost 50 million Americans tuned in to see Barbara Walters's exclusive March 1999 television interview with

Monica Lewinsky on ABC's *20/20*, despite numerous polls in the preceding months suggesting the public had had its fill of news about the former White House aide.[9] While there may be a certain amount of truth to this argument, it misses one key point: Increases in readership and television viewing measured against usual audience size are relatively small shifts, since the overall growth in circulation and network TV audiences stagnated long ago. In other words, the increased audience for scandal coverage is by and large an increase among the relatively small subset of the population who are already news consumers, not the growing number of news "disconnecteds" who have already turned off or tuned out.

"Gotcha" journalism is not the driving force behind these diminishing news audiences. But news coverage driven by values contrary to the public's only contributes to the public's sense that the media does not share their interests. Journalists themselves are beginning to recognize this as a problem. In the aforementioned Pew poll, more than half of news professionals surveyed—57 percent nationally and 51 percent locally—agreed that "journalists have become out-of-touch with their audiences."[10]

Personal scrutiny also ensures that journalists are quite literally "out of touch" with some of the figures they cover. One immediate consequence of political journalists' increased focus on the private lives of politicians is decreased access. In 1998, Idaho representative Helen Chenoweth challenged a news story in the *Spokane Spokesman-Review*, which reported that she had lied in denying an affair with a married business partner. (She was asked about it directly by a reporter during an interview in a previous campaign.) Later, when the *Spokesman-Review* sought to interview Chenoweth for other news stories and profiles, she said she was too busy. "I know my staff was just looking out for my best interests as far as my time," she said, dismissing a reporter's questions about her interview policy after a candidate debate late in the campaign.[11]

The losers in Chenoweth's feud with the *Spokesman-Review* were not the publication's reporters but the representative's constituents who read the newspaper and depend on it to relay their questions and her answers. However, there was no public outcry about Chenoweth's refusal to answer the newspaper's questions. In fact, she was reelected to a third term with 55 percent of the vote. The *Spokesman-Review* was right to report the discrepancies between its reporter's notes and Chenoweth's claim that she had never lied about her relationship. Nonetheless, the public will not side with reporters who they think are only interested in asking questions that they have no interest in seeing answered. This puts reporters and editors in an impossible bind.

The mission of the popular press is not to be popular. And in blaming the press for the sins about which it reports, the public—and even some critics—may be shooting the messenger. But ignoring public attitudes about press behavior could have grave consequences for the media as well as the political process. In combination with court rulings and high jury awards against reporters and declining public support for First Amendment press rights, diminished public confidence in the media poses more than a business threat to journalism's future. It is a potential threat to the very idea of an unrestricted press that was key to the nation's founding, its survival, and its future. Meanwhile, readers and viewers may increasingly turn to alternative sources of information (described in chapter 2) for pseudonews that does not stand up to traditional journalistic standards of balance and accuracy. Reporters, editors and producers cannot be stubborn or cavalier about public attitudes. Ignoring these threats is as self-destructive as the reckless personal behavior of politicians that today's journalists so meticulously document.

So far, the threats to journalism's future and the tabloid-ization of political coverage are not causing news organizations to hemorrhage talent. As with elected office itself, ambition al-most guarantees that there will be hungry, talented young report-ers interested in covering politics and government. These high-profile beats are still prime assignments in most newsrooms. More generally, journalism still provides opportunities to watch history being made and to get to know those who make it.

Nonetheless, some prominent national journalists have left their daily beats to try to reform their profession and the pro-cess of political discourse. Some have become nonprofit crusad-ers for better media. For example, former *Washington Post* political reporter Paul Taylor joined former CBS News anchor-man Walter Cronkite before the 1996 presidential race to mount their own campaign to convince the major television networks to give free airtime to candidates. Tom Rosenstiel, a former re-porter for the *Los Angeles Times* and *Newsweek*, now serves as director of the Project for Excellence in Journalism and vice chairman of the Committee of Concerned Journalists, where he has led efforts to raise standards and organize support for sen-sible journalistic reforms.

Some news organizations have embraced a new kind of social responsibility journalism, championed by the Pew Cen-ter for Civic Journalism, a nonprofit initiative financed by the Pew Charitable Trusts. No longer willing merely to report the news, some journalists see it as their duty to improve American society. This kind of reporting—which often uses extensive poll-ing, focus groups, voter interviews and public forums to define an editorial agenda—represents a well-intentioned desire by journalists to reconnect with their audience. However, it is also a manifestation of the same editorial idealism that has led to the press emphasis on "character questions." Ultimately, journalism that does not reflect its audience's interests will lose that audience. But it is risky to assume that journalists will be any more successful at representing their readers and viewers when reporting on issues of public concern than they have been when reporting on the private lives of elected officials. These well-meaning journalistic experiments, with their potential to reengage the public, deserve careful attention and close scrutiny.

At the same time, the interactive nature of Internet journalism is pushing some for-profit online news operations in the same direction as the new civic journalists. These online editorial experiments, involving such unconventional media forces as America Online (AOL) and Yahoo!, also have potential to change the direction of mainstream reporting—and are attracting innovative and reform-minded talent from the ranks of traditional journalism. Former ABC News political reporter and Pentagon spokeswoman Kathleen deLaski went to America Online in 1996 to try to develop a new kind of political communication. The idea of covering politics in the interactive medium that AOL offered was enticing "because I thought political journalism could be better when the consumer is choosing what he/she wants to learn," deLaski said. At the same time, the former broadcast reporter said working online was a welcome alternative to the direction of political news on television:

> I went to AOL because I felt I was not serving the viewing audience well when I was on the campaign trail as a TV reporter. I would pick the five sentences of description each day and two sound bites that I could cram into my one-minute and thirty-second spot for ABC News to sum up the candidate's day. The stories often

began, "Dogged by the polls. . . ." If you watched one of my stories, you had no idea what the candidate stood for. You learned how his day went versus the other guy's day.[12]

Editorial experimentation in the nonprofit and corporate worlds offers evidence that some thoughtful journalists recognize the problems in their profession and are devoting their careers to addressing them. News organizations must be careful not to drive journalism's "best and brightest" reformers from their ranks.

One unanticipated consequence of media overcoverage of politicians' personal lives is a desensitizing effect among readers and viewers. Eventually, the public will tune out coverage of stories about which it has little interest, no matter how big the headlines or how prominent the TV news reports, as public reaction to the Monica Lewinsky scandal demonstrated. Even private behavior of legitimate public concern can fade into a mix of sensational news, like the blur of celebrity headlines on the cover of a supermarket tabloid. Revelations that once doomed candidacies and careers (such as Republican Nelson Rockefeller's divorce or Democrat Gary Hart's liaisons) are shrugged off later, as was the case with Republican Bob Dole's affair before his first divorce and President Clinton's Oval Office escapades. To some, this effect shows growing maturity on the part of voters and the press. But it also suggests a dangerous opportunity for politicians to exploit the public's scandal fatigue and convince voters to overlook failings that should raise legitimate questions about their fitness to serve.

The public itself has little time or interest in modern politics. By focusing so much attention on the personal lives of public servants, the press squanders what little chance it has to engage the electorate, to remind voters about the connections between public policy and their own personal lives. Voters are willing to devote only so much time to the study of politics. If coverage of personal politics dominates the news, then the public learns less about the matters that ought to be foremost in their minds when they vote. The less informed voters are when they walk into their polling places, the greater the chance that they will elect people who should not be in public office. The election of a real political cad or scoundrel would be the most tragic and ironic consequence of a media process that is intended to protect the public from just such a decision.

6

The Muck Stops Here

While the press is often guilty of trespassing into the private lives of politicians, there are enough instances of restraint to justify the hope that this repeat offender is not beyond rehabilitation. Journalism's best practices can ensure fair coverage, even when a politician's private life is the subject of legitimate news interest. In the case of 1996 Republican presidential nominee Bob Dole, for example, the *Washington Post* and other major national publications initially refrained from publishing confirmed reports about an extramarital affair in the candidate's past. Yet the eventual coverage of Dole's long-ago affair also shows how competitive forces can effectively override good editorial decisions. It also is a reminder of the murky "news judgments" that often guide editors.

A week before Dole accepted his party's nomination, the *Post* ran a front-page story on the former Senate majority leader's abrupt 1972 divorce. The story by staff writer Kevin Merida was based in large part on unpublished interviews with Dole's former wife, Phyllis Macey. *Post* investigative reporter Bob Woodward conducted the interviews with another journalist during the previous year for Woodward's book *The Choice*. Macey was still at a loss to explain the surprising demise of her marriage of more than twenty-three years. "You'd have to ask him those questions," she told Woodward. "I was pretty stunned."[1]

Dole would not speak to the *Post*, but other sources emerged soon after the newspaper published Merida's story on August 7. Based on calls prompted by the article, the newspaper soon learned that Dole began an extramarital affair with a Washington woman in the late 1960s, four years before the divorce. "We knew nothing at that time about this other relationship" before the Merida story ran, said executive editor Leonard Downie Jr. "It was as a result of running that story that we got a tip about the other relationship."[2]

Whether to publish what the *Post* ultimately confirmed about the affair was the subject of lengthy debate among the newspaper's top editors. Then–managing editor Robert G. Kaiser was among those who favored publication. Kaiser argued that the Republican Party had "staked out a position on family values" that made Dole's past affair relevant to his supporters. Kaiser also said the story was relevant because "there's no statute of limitations on presidential candidates." Downie, on the other hand, argued that an affair that began almost three decades earlier "did not meet our standards for the publication of information about the private lives of public officials." Downie spiked the story.[3]

Journalists at *Time* magazine uncovered the Dole story separately and came to similar conclusions about its news value. *Time* managing editor Walter Isaacson decided that Dole's past affair was not news at such a late date in the election cycle, despite corroborating evidence from Dole's mistress.

> She had provided evidence that the Dole folks privately were not contradicting. Perhaps in a different context—as part of an overall bio of him done at the beginning of a campaign—we could have considered it a valid thing to mention in passing in the larger context of his life and

background. But as a story on its own coming a week or two before the election, it did not seem truly relevant to his character at the time, and we'd have just been doing it for the momentary sensation. So it did not seem valid, and we did not do it.[4]

The *New York Daily News*, however, did not share the *Post*'s and *Time*'s qualms. It published a story on the former senator's late-1960s romance a week before the tabloid *National Enquirer* ran its own version. When reporters asked Dole publicly about those reports, the candidate snapped back, "You're as bad as they are," referring scornfully to the tabloid report. Dole's campaign also issued a statement that carefully avoided the issue of his adultery. Instead, Dole's campaign focused on the *Enquirer* report itself, borrowing a technique perfected by Bill Clinton's spin team in 1992, when the *Star* tabloid first reported on Gennifer Flowers's affair with the Arkansas governor. "Last week the *National Enquirer* published stories on deep sea-diving monkeys and a cross-dressing school teacher," a campaign spokesman said. "Next week, they will trash Bob Dole. Maybe there were no UFO sightings to occupy their attentions. By publishing trashing gossip from over two decades ago just days before the election, the *National Enquirer* failed to meet even the low standards it sets for itself. If your news organization wants to follow the *National Enquirer*'s lead, you may do so without the Dole campaign's help."[5]

Several news organizations covered Dole's response to reports about his affair, including the *Washington Post*. "When a candidate for president is asked questions in a public press conference about something and responds to them, it's very difficult to ignore them if we think that they would matter to our readers," Downie explained.[6] That was a reversal of the *Post*'s earlier decision not to publish what it knew about the affair. But Downie emphasized that the newspaper was careful with how it "played" the story, running the information at the end of a long, run-of-the-mill campaign story, omitting details of the affair, including the woman's name. Downie also spoke on the record in the article about the *Post*'s original decision not to publish the story and explained why the newspaper was changing course.[7] Looking back, Downie said those editorial and placement decisions were an intentional effort to put the news about the GOP nominee in its proper context:

> The way in which we report [a story] also makes a difference, which I think journalists don't often recognize as well as readers do. Readers take the front page seriously. They take story length seriously. They take play seriously. So the mere mention of something is not the same thing as how you play it. So you can disseminate information that you think is now necessary, that your readers would want you to disseminate to them, but do it with perspective. Let them see the perspective you place on it by play.[8]

Downie said his newspaper "would never run a story based on a *National Enquirer* story." Running a story based on a candidate's indirect response to a *National Enquirer* report is a subtle distinction that might be lost on most readers. However, Downie's comments and the *Post*'s overall handling of the Dole story show that there are constructive ways of dealing with sensitive personal material, even in the face of powerful competitive pressures. The *Post* based its original decision not to run the Dole story on its own news judgment after a wide-ranging editorial debate. Downie's decision was based on facts investigated thoroughly by his staff, not on mere gossip. When Dole's response to other news reports about the affair made the newspaper's editors reevaluate their decision, Downie spoke clearly and directly to his readers about the *Post*'s reasoning. And by playing the news deep on the "jump" page of an otherwise routine campaign story, rather than as a front-page story with its own headline, Downie used the power of layout and story placement to put the information about Dole into context. The *Post*'s process on the Dole story provides a template for news decision-making on sensitive stories about the private lives of political figures.

Can that template be translated into standards of behavior for the press itself?

THE FAIRNESS DOCTRINE

Certain journalistic conventions are widely accepted. For example, most news organizations do not identify rape victims and only rarely name juveniles accused of crimes. Yet many editors resist setting blanket rules on what the press should and should not report about politicians, such as a statute of limitations on a candidate's past affairs. Guidelines such as the "fairness doctrine" outlined in chapter 1 provide a useful starting point for editors struggling with decisions over the relevance of an extramarital dalliance or other details in a political figure's private life, past or present.

Some stories, we contend, should remain out of bounds in most circumstances. Among them:

- Internal family matters such as child rearing and other nonlegal issues involving the candidate's family and underage children
- Current extramarital sexual activity that is discreet,

legal, and not in conflict with an official's public responsibilities
- Past sexual activity and personal relationships that occurred many years earlier
- Sexual orientation
- Youthful indulgence or experimentation with drugs and alcohol

These guidelines, which editors must apply to news stories on a case-by-case basis, offer reasonable limits for journalists as well as healthy zones of privacy for those who enter political life. At the same time, our fairness doctrine leaves plenty of room for reasonable scrutiny of those who seek the public's trust. Among the areas left open for investigation are:

- Personal and professional finances
- Health issues
- Legal questions, both civil and criminal
- Sexual activity that is compulsive, manifestly indiscreet, and/or clearly in conflict with an official's public responsibilities
- Current alcohol and drug abuse or other debilitating behavior
- Any illegal drug use that would violate government hiring practices that an official or candidate would be responsible for enforcing
- Any private behavior that involves the use of public funds or taxpayer-subsidized facilities in a substantial way

While none of the behaviors described here should automatically disqualify a candidate from public office, they are legitimate areas for journalistic investigation and voter scrutiny.

PUBLIC CHARACTER

Another legitimate subject for press inquiry is a candidate's public character. How political figures relate to their staffs and peers is at least as important as how they relate to friends and family members. One example of such coverage was reporting in the fall of 1999 about Arizona senator John McCain's legendary temper. A front-page story in the *New York Times* on the Republican presidential candidate's "sometimes prickly personality" relied heavily on accounts by Arizona governor Jane Dee Hull, a fellow Republican who had endorsed McCain rival George W. Bush. During an interview with a *Times* reporter, Hull demonstrated how she would hold the phone away from her ear during the senator's occasional tirades. "You've got to hold it out there for a while, and let him calm down," Hull said. "We all have our faults, and it's something that John has to keep control of." The *Arizona Republic*—which was often the subject of McCain's ire—chimed in with a follow-up editorial asking whether the senator was temperamentally suited to the presidency. "If McCain is truly a serious contender for the presidency, it is time the rest of the nation learn about the John McCain we know in Arizona," the editorial said.[9]

The reporting and commentary on McCain's temper was at least as revealing and useful to voters as reporters' earlier questions about his admitted womanizing before his 1980 divorce from his first wife. Yet reporters rarely probe this kind of "character question," even when such matters are fairly easily documented. Candidate Bill Clinton, whose volcanic temper rivals McCain's, did not get the same scrutiny in 1992, when reporters covering his campaign witnessed and even videotaped his tantrums. Clinton exploded at the press, his enemies, low-level staff aides—all within view or earshot of journalists and TV cameras. While the press reported many of these incidents, little ink or airtime was devoted to Clinton's pattern of behavior until after the election, when the president-elect berated a staff aide for allowing photographers to get near him on the golf course. Three months later, Clinton dressed down another aide for trying to block two local dignitaries from attending a Washington, D.C., photo opportunity. While these little-covered scenes might not have changed the direction of the 1992 campaign, they offered a revealing contrast to Clinton's public image as a compassionate listener. Whether such behavior was relevant to voters was a subjective question that journalists answered for their readers and viewers by deciding not to tell the whole story about Clinton's eruptions until after the election.[10]

Other issues also deserve greater attention than they ordinarily receive from the media's character cops. A candidate's management skills, his or her ego, how a candidate handles stress, advice or a setback are all issues that deserve examination, even if they rarely generate scandal or controversy.

CURBING FEEDING FRENZIES

To be credible, news coverage of a political scandal must be commensurate with the offense. Offering readers or viewers more than they can reasonably consume in a single day on a regular basis is excessive. President Clinton's reckless sexual relationship with a White House intern, for example, was a big story by almost every measure. The affair jeopardized Clinton's administration, tarred his reputation and legacy, and produced the second presidential impeachment trial in American history. Yet the public's distaste for the Lewinsky story, at least as measured by polls, was in some ways a reaction to the media's protracted and excessive coverage of the allegations, especially early in the investigation.

Research compiled by the Center for Media and Public
Affairs found that the nightly news shows on the three major
broadcast networks produced 183 stories on Monica Lewinsky
in just the first ten days of the scandal in 1998. Over the entire
year, ABC's, CBS's and NBC's evening news shows produced
1,636 Lewinsky stories. That eclipsed the networks' *combined*
coverage of that year's military standoff with Iraq, the economic
crises in Asia and Russia, the bombing of two U.S. embassies
in Africa, the Israeli–Palestinian peace process, nuclear weapons
tests by India and Pakistan, and the ethnic conflict in Kosovo
that led the United States to war the following year. The 642
evening news stories on the standoff with Iraq over United Na-
tions' weapons inspections also included 42 stories that mentioned the so-called *Wag the Dog* scenario—a reference to a
1998 movie about a White House spin team that "produces" a
war to divert public attention from a presidential sex scandal.[11]

Newspaper editors were just as focused on the Lewinsky
story as TV news producers were. The *New York Times* and the
Washington Post regularly offered readers more than a dozen
stories a day on the topic in 1998 and during the impeachment
trial in early 1999. The volume of coverage generated by a story
like the Lewinsky investigation conveys a sense of media obses-
sion to readers and viewers that overwhelms even legitimate
interest in a topic. Story placement—or misplacement—also
contributes to the perception of overkill. Prominence is a powerful tool for signaling the significance of a story to readers and
viewers. But excessive front-page and top-of-the-newscast play
for one story over time takes away an editor's or producer's
ability to convey the relative importance of news developments.
Kaiser, the former *Washington Post* managing editor, defended
the newspaper's overall coverage of the impeachment process,
but said some elements of the investigation were overplayed on

the newspaper's front page. "I'm sure that if we were forced to relive the entire Monica story, we'd have the most guilt about decisions of that kind."[12]

The number of reporters that editors and producers assign to stories is another important factor in managing a feeding frenzy. While any newsroom manager's inclination is to mobilize all of his or her forces in response to a big story, news about the private lives of political figures is often covered at levels that far exceed other significant political developments, such as the passage of a landmark piece of legislation. When Colorado governor Roy Romer held a news conference to explain his "affectionate" relationship with a longtime aide and adviser, the *Denver Post* ran almost a dozen articles, columns and sidebars the next day, including news stories written by at least nine reporters. *Denver Post* editor Dennis Britton said it is difficult, if not impossible, for editors to resist sending out as many reporters as they can to cover a big story, whether it is the Romer relationship at the state level or the Lewinsky investigation at the national level. But Britton said senior editors have a responsibility to their readers to exercise news judgment and ensure that the subsequent coverage reflects the actual significance of the event, not the pride of the reporters and assignment editors who may have worked hard to nail down every angle. "You don't have to give everybody a byline," Britton said. "You don't have to soothe everybody's ego. That's why we're called gatekeepers."[13]

RESISTING RUMORS

The changing nature of the news business, detailed in chapter 2, suggests a need for new approaches to making difficult editorial decisions about widespread, unconfirmed political rumors. In today's highly competitive media market, political gossip can take root and spread like kudzu, especially via alternative news routes, such as the Internet, talk radio and even late-night television comedy. *Time* magazine's Walter Isaacson says all this can be tempting fodder for journalists:

> One difficulty, in general, is how to handle stories that are moving up the food chain, from a [Matt] Drudge to a tabloid to cable and radio talk shows and eventually into the mainstream. Although it's important to resist the tabloid creep, sometimes it becomes perverse not to analyze a story that everyone already knows about and is talking about. In such cases, it's important to try to put the thing in perspective and resist being part of a braying pack chasing each salacious detail.[14]

In the 1994 book *When Should the Watchdogs Bark?*, authors Sabato and Lichter described three approaches the mainstream press used to cover early allegations of sexual misconduct by President Clinton.[15] All three options also apply to general news coverage of most politically sensitive personal rumors and innuendo. They are:

- The "See No Evil" Approach: Pretend that a rumor does not exist—long the preferred treatment for unconfirmed political gossip or rumors that reporters completely disbelieve. However, least-common-denominator journalism and competitive forces often spread the gossip anyway.
- The Minimalist Approach: Allude to the gossip in print or on the air without confirming or disproving the substance of the allegation, as in a self-reflective media story

about how reporters are debating how to handle a sensitive rumor. This is the most common journalistic approach when a political figure denies or makes another statement about a rumor or when competing media circulate an allegation. That a rumor is "out there" being discussed in political circles, even if no one will discuss it on the record, is enough of a fact on which to base a news story in this model.

- The Investigative Approach: The least common but most healthy of all the journalistic options requires reporters to actually work to confirm or refute a rumor, or at the very least detail the substance on which the gossip is based. This is also the most difficult and time-consuming option.

Many news organizations vacillate between the "see no evil" approach and the investigative option: Once a rumor begins to circulate publicly, journalists will sometimes detail their previous reporting on the subject, even if it is not conclusive. Editors at the *New York Daily News* applied this "what we knew and when we knew it" approach to Rudolph Giuliani after a 1997 *Vanity Fair* magazine profile alleged an extramarital affair between the married mayor and his communications director. A *Daily News* article said that *Vanity Fair*'s story "threw into public light reports of marital difficulties that had been the subject of investigations by various media outlets, including the *Daily News*, but had not been sufficiently substantiated for publication." Another report in the newspaper said its sources on the rumors "all demanded anonymity and none had firsthand knowledge of the state of the mayor's marriage or the alleged liaison."[16]

The *Daily News* stories did not say whether rumors about Giuliani's marriage were true, but they did convey to readers the substance of the newspaper's own reporting and its editors' evaluation of the information's reliability. The statements also explained to readers why the newspaper did not previously report the rumors. The *Daily News* went on to probe the substance of the *Vanity Fair* story, finding travel records that appeared to contradict key points of the magazine's assertions about Giuliani's alleged romance. *Vanity Fair* editor Graydon Carter later conceded "minor errors" in his magazine's account, but he stood by the story.[17]

In South Carolina that same year, the *State* newspaper in Columbia was even more detailed in summarizing its investigation of rumors about Republican governor David Beasley. When a political rival began circulating unsubstantiated stories about an alleged affair between the governor and his spokeswoman, the newspaper did an entire story on the rumors, which it said were "investigated by all the state's major news organizations. Reporters found no evidence that Beasley has been unfaithful to his wife. The *State* found that every rumor that included a specific place or date or other element that could be verified failed to check out." A year later, when South Carolina Democrats tried to make the rumor an issue in Beasley's campaign for a second term, the journalist who wrote the 1997 story on the *State*'s investigation once again detailed her reporting in a long opinion column. (See exhibit B to read the text of Cindi Ross Scoppe's editorial.)[18]

Editors are often reluctant to employ the investigative approach, especially when rumors remain unconfirmed or appear to be untrue, because they fear that these stories serve as a vehicle for spreading the gossip. But in a highly competitive, multimedia era in which voters obtain information about political candidates from numerous sources, mainstream media organizations have an increasing obligation to open their notebooks and help their readers and viewers sort fact from fiction and news from gossip. In addition, the substance of this reporting must be repeated continuously, especially when it comes to unfounded rumors, in order to offset the effects of elevating and spreading the gossip. It is not enough to report in one comprehensive story that the substance of a widespread rumor is impossible to confirm or demonstrably false. Journalists must repeat those conclusions to their readers and viewers as often as they repeat the rumors themselves.

SPEAK FOR THE STORY ITSELF

Those who think the political press has a lot of explaining to do are right. Survey after survey on the media shows that the public ascribes a variety of motives to media decisions about politicians and their private behavior. Partisan or personal bias, scandal-mongering commercialism and pure cynicism are all suspected. Journalists go a long way in helping consumers understand their judgments, standards and practices simply by stating them clearly. News stories no longer speak for themselves. The editors and producers who assign and approve them must find outlets to do the speaking for them.

In newspapers, editors have a number of tools for conveying the thoughts behind an editorial decision, including sidebars, editor's notes, editorials and columns, even quotes from the editor within a news story. Each method has its advantages, but short sidebar articles or editor's notes provide the greatest flexibility as well as the highest visibility in proximity to the main text. Some editors are reluctant to use these devices because they fear their comments would be an open acknowledgment that their news decisions directly affect the political process. In fact, by providing readers with a justification for a subjective news judgment, these devices do serve as an admission that journalists are far more than mere objective observers sitting on the sidelines of modern politics. A contemporary editor must be willing to recognize that reality and talk honestly with his or her readers about its ramifications.

The *Boston Globe* attempted to explain its decision to write about former Boston mayor Raymond L. Flynn's drinking habits in a news sidebar to its lengthy front-page story on the possible Massachusetts governor candidate in 1997. The sidebar did not directly quote *Globe* reporters or editors but included statements from a number of journalism professors and ethicists on the relevance of a political candidate's drinking. It also offered a two-paragraph explanation of the standards that the newspaper said guide most journalists on such questions: "These inexact guideposts require judging the impact, extent, and frequency of a public official's or candidate's drinking, and knowing whether it's done publicly or privately. . . . Finally, the more important the office someone holds or seeks to hold, the higher the level of scrutiny becomes."[19]

The *Idaho Statesman* in Boise was even more direct in providing its readers an explanation of its actions in September 1998, when it broke a story about Representative Helen Chenoweth's affair with a married man while she was a single woman in the 1980s, before her election to Congress. The *Statesman* broke the story two days after the Republican congressman, who hated to be called a congresswoman, began airing a series of television ads about President Clinton's relationship with Monica Lewinsky. "I believe that personal conduct and integrity does matter," Chenoweth said in one spot. Editors at the *Statesman* decided Chenoweth's statements about Clinton's affair gave them reason to investigate long-standing rumors that she had had a six-year relationship with her former business partner, an ex–state legislator who twice ran for governor of Idaho. In a statement, Chenoweth admitted the relationship to the newspaper and insisted that her "comments regarding the president are completely consistent." In fact, Chenoweth's relationship would have fallen completely outside the statute of limitations for such a story under the guidelines suggested here, if not for her comments on the president.

An editor's note accompanying the *Statesman*'s story explained that the newspaper decided to report the relationship "after considerable deliberation" because of Chenoweth's TV ads. "Our decision reflects the fact that she made 'personal conduct' an accountability issue," the note said.[20] In a separate editorial five days later, *Statesman* editor Karen Baker wrote a detailed account of the newspaper's decision-making process, including its word choice and its reasons for playing the story below the fold on the front page (so that it would not be visible in street-corner news racks). Baker repeated the editor's note explanation that the newspaper felt Chenoweth had made her affair an issue with her television campaign:

> Reporters and editors routinely hear rumors about newsmakers and, in particular, candidates for office. Many of them we do not even bother to try to check out, because there is no public issue involved. . . . We decided to print the [Chenoweth] story only after a series of conversations with editors, reporters and the publisher. We weighed the possible consequences of publishing and not publishing, and considered the pain the story would cause those individuals involved. The scales tipped in favor of going with the story.[21]

One could quibble with the *Statesman*'s arguments, as Chenoweth did. Hypocrisy, after all, is in the eye of the beholder. But if all readers and all viewers received such clear accounting of how the news arrived on their doorsteps and appeared on their television screens, public opinion of journalism might soar. (See exhibit B for the complete text of Baker's editorial.)

CHECKS AND BALANCES

Encouraging the behavior and enforcing the standards described above is difficult in a profession as decentralized as journalism. The press rarely holds itself to the same standards as the people and institutions it covers. Journalists view self-regulating industries or unchecked government powers with suspicion. Yet few major news organizations have appointed independent ombudsmen to address reader complaints and stand watch over journalism's few articulated rules and practices, including those that apply to the private lives of public figures.

Ombudsmen—also known as reader representatives, reader advocates and public editors—are an increasingly common fixture in modern newsrooms. The *Courier Journal* and the *Louisville Times* in Kentucky established the first U.S. newspaper ombudsman in 1967. After more than three decades, more than thirty U.S. newspapers are represented in the membership of Organization of News Ombudsmen, including such large-circulation industry leaders as the *Arizona Republic*, the *Boston Globe*, the *Chicago Tribune*, the *Los Angeles Times*, the *Miami Herald*, the *Orange County Register*, the *Philadelphia Inquirer*, the *Portland Oregonian*, the *San Diego Union-Tribune*, and the *Washington Post*. Yet hundreds of other newspapers have resisted appointing editors whose jobs are to represent readers' tastes and opinions in newsrooms, as well as in print. On-air discussions about television news decisions, even a brief weekly commentary by an appointed viewer representative, would enhance the credibility of broadcast and cable newscasts. However, television stations and networks have been even slower than newspapers to adopt the ombudsman practice.

There are many arguments against appointing ombudsmen, which *Portland Oregonian* public editor Michele McLellan summarized succinctly in a 1998 column on the topic:

> Much resistance to having ombudsmen in media outlets hinges on the fear that self-criticism undermines credibility. Legal concerns (that self-criticism will give ammunition to potential litigants) and practical considerations (that perhaps the staff position would be better used to hire an additional reporter or photographer) also figure. Some editors argue that they are their own ombudsmen. And ideally, everyone on every newsroom staff or editorial board would have the time and the fair-mindedness to effectively deal with criticisms of their work.[22]

These arguments aside, people in the news business should understand the need for fair-minded detachment better than most. When chosen from a newsroom's senior staff or from leadership positions in other news organizations, ombudsmen often have the clout to serve as a powerful emergency brake on journalism's worst excesses, including intrusive and unnecessary coverage of political leaders.

News coverage of the media itself also serves as a deterrent to journalism that crosses that line, especially when high-caliber reporters such as Bill Powers of *National Journal* and Howard Kurtz of the *Washington Post* and CNN are allowed to focus intensely on the errors and limitations of their colleagues—even their own newsrooms. But media reporting can also become a dangerous vehicle for a kind of "meta-journalism" that repeats rumors or gossip that might not otherwise be fit to print or broadcast, as in stories that detail how "editors across Washington" are struggling with difficult journalistic quandaries. While this book necessarily relies heavily on these accounts, routine reporting about the media should not be a back door through which stories that would not otherwise reach a newsroom's standards are allowed to pass.

The media elite often seems removed from the average news consumer who buys a daily newspaper or a weekly news-magazine and watches the occasional news show. But those elites are far more closely tied to average citizens than they themselves believe or would want to admit. In the end, the news establishment depends on casual news readers and viewers to support their empires, many of which are already on shaky financial ground. That being true, news executives must be responsive to reasonable and thoughtful public opinion whenever it is mani-fested. (Many outside the news business are surprised to discover just how few letters or calls it can take to change a newspaper's policy about this or a TV station's approach to that.)

The obverse relationship deserves emphasis. Citizens have the responsibility to shake off the tendency to be mere specta-tors and passive news receptacles. In a democracy, whether we like it or not, whether it is the ideal or not, citizens themselves must set the rules and, even more critically, enforce those rules with their eyes, their ears, and their pocketbooks.

Public standards and news standards do not always corre-spond, and public opinion should not substitute for news judg-ment. But public accountability can be a force that helps guide editorial decision-makers through their most difficult questions about what is news and what is not.

Exhibit A

Case Studies

The media case studies that follow briefly summarize how national and local news organizations handled the key stories that are the focus of this book. Many of these summaries contain political gossip and rumor, often denied, unsubstantiated and even provably false. We have graded the decision to publish or broadcast each of these stories A to F based on our "fairness doctrine" detailed in chapter 1. The summaries are presented here roughly in chronological order.

David Funderburk: A car accident in 1995 cost the Republican congressman from North Carolina a $25 fine, court expenses, and a second term in the House of Representatives. Funderburk and his wife insisted she was driving when their car forced a van off a remote stretch of highway, injuring two adults and their four-year-old daughter. Witnesses at the scene said that the congressman was in fact behind the wheel and switched places with his wife after driving a half-mile down the road from the accident. To put the matter to rest, the former Eagle Scout pleaded no contest to a minor traffic offense. A year later, Funderburk's Democratic rival used the incident in a damning television ad in a successful campaign to oust the GOP freshman.

The car accident was a legal/police matter involving the candidate and his family. Accusations in a political campaign also deserve explanation.

The Gore Family: The son of a United States senator, Vice President Al Gore has often spoken about his own children in his campaigns, most famously in his speech at the 1992 Democratic National Convention, when he spoke movingly about the traffic accident that almost killed his son, Albert III. Gore's wife, Tipper, has also written and spoken extensively on the subject of child rearing and parenthood. While not in any way unusual in politics, the Gores' public statements about their family have cost their children some of the privacy generally afforded to other children of prominent public figures.

Dozens of media outlets across the country carried news wire reports and commentary about Sarah Gore after police cited the sixteen-year-old for holding an open beer can in a car outside a suburban Washington high school party in 1995. The police did not release Sarah Gore's name, but the vice president's family acknowledged the incident in a public statement asking for privacy. When an interviewer asked Tipper Gore about the incident live on Fox *Morning News* a few days later, she repeated her family's request.

Coverage of a politician's underage children is generally unfair. Although the police involvement and the Gore family statement made the story difficult to ignore, the story got far more play than it deserved.

The press was sympathetic to the Gores' requests for privacy a year later, when Albert III transferred private schools after a disciplinary incident at St. Albans, a prestigious private school for boys and the vice president's alma mater. Rumors about the vice president's son circulated widely in Washington. Several news organizations investigated but did not report on the incident involving the seventh-grade student, even after a detailed but unsourced account in *Washingtonian* magazine suggested that Albert III was caught with marijuana. Several reporters who investigated the story said there was no police involvement and no evidence that the Gores used their position to get their son out of trouble. The Gores also made no public statement about the incident, as they had when their daughter got in trouble, although the vice president contacted at least one news organization, the Capitol Hill newspaper *Roll Call*, to try to headoff reporters' inquiries. (In the case of each reporter we interviewed, editors decided not to run the information before stories were written and the reporting was complete, so some details of the incident have not been publicly reported.)

 The Gore children's visible role in their parents' public life made them a legitimate news story, so press restraint on this story about a politician's underage child is an encouraging reminder that there still are some news standards, despite Washingtonian's *story.*

Chelsea Clinton: Bill and Hillary Clinton have had better luck then the Gores in protecting their daughter from media attention. But the Clintons' convenient use of their daughter as a political prop, including a 1992 cover story for *People* magazine orchestrated by Bill Clinton's presidential campaign, occasionally contravened their public requests for Chelsea's privacy.

The long Monica Lewinsky investigation increased tabloid and mainstream press interest in Chelsea's role in the first family. Accounts of Chelsea's health problems and dating life at Stanford University infuriated her parents, as did a 1998 cover story on the first daughter—ironically in *People* magazine.

 Chelsea Clinton's role in her parents' public life made her a legitimate news story, but her personal life and health were a nonlegal matter that did not deserve coverage. However, the Clintons brought some of the press attention on themselves with their use of their daughter as a convenient political tool.

Alma Powell: The wife of Colin Powell was a reluctant recruit in the fight to convince the former Army general and chairman of the Joint Chiefs of Staff to run for president in 1996. In October 1995, deep in a story about Powell's decision-making process, reporters for the *Philadelphia Inquirer* reported that Alma Powell had been treated for clinical depression. A week later *Newsweek* repeated the same information, giving the news slightly more prominent play than the *Inquirer*. While both the *Inquirer* and *Newsweek* stories reported Alma Powell's medical treatment in the context of longer profiles, other news organizations speculated that such unwelcome scrutiny of the Powells' family life would drive the general from the race. But when Powell took himself out of the running at a November 1995 news conference, he spoke matter-of-factly about Alma's treatment (comparing it to his treatment for high blood pressure) and said the stories about his wife were not a factor in his decision not to run.

Powell's depression fell into the category of nonlegal matters involving the candidate's family. The Powells' openness, while good public relations and a noble effort to destigmatize a common illness, also encourages similar press scrutiny of others.

John Kasich: Rumors that Republican congressman John Kasich of Ohio was gay started during the House Budget Committee chairman's 1996 reelection campaign and lasted throughout his brief run for his party's 2000 presidential nomination. In the 1996 race, Kasich's Democratic rival sought a Justice Department investigation of the congressman, alleging a conflict of interest because he shared the lease on a Washington-area townhouse with his well-paid male chief of staff. The shared lease was not unusual, even among congressmen, who must maintain residences in their home districts as well as Washington. Kasich, who was divorced at the time, accused his opponent of trying to smear him with an unspoken suggestion of homosexuality. Local media chided the Democrat, but the rumor nevertheless got national attention that fall in a *Time* magazine story.

 The 1996 accusation by a political opponent deserved to be reported, and news accounts properly noted that the allegation was not substantiated. But ongoing circulation of an unproven rumor after the 1996 campaign served no journalistic purpose. While the alleged relationship involved a staff member, the financial arrangement was not unusual. Also, sexuality per se is not newsworthy.

Jim Kolbe: Arizona congressman Jim Kolbe "outed" himself in 1996, declaring his homosexuality in a statement released to the media before his preference was reported in the *Advocate*, a national gay newspaper. Kolbe's homosexuality was long rumored in Arizona politics, especially among gay rights activists, even before the divorced, two-term congressman released his statement. Kolbe's record on gay rights issues was mixed. He did not side dogmatically with activists on either side of the issue. His July 1996 vote for a GOP bill that allowed states to refuse to sanction homosexual marriages angered some gay leaders, prompting the *Advocate* article on the congressman's alleged hypocrisy. Kolbe's announcement made him only the fourth openly gay member of Congress at the time.

The congressman made his own public announcement in a press release covered by Arizona and national media. Kolbe's brother, an Arizona political columnist, also wrote about the congressman's decision to acknowledge his sexuality. The Advocate *article that prompted the congressman's statement was based on a debatable link between his private life and public actions. (One's position on gay marriage and the related state's rights issues are not necessarily dependent on one's own sexuality, just as women and minorities may disagree on affirmative action.)*

Bob Dole: Late in the 1996 presidential campaign, several news organizations determined that Republican nominee Bob Dole, the former Senate majority leader, had a four-year extramarital affair before his 1972 divorce from his first wife. Both *Time* magazine and the *Washington Post* decided independently not to run stories about the affair, despite an on-the-record confirmation from the Washington-area woman involved. The *Post* and other news organizations eventually did report some details of the twenty-four-year-old romance after the *New York Daily News* published its own account and Dole began facing questions from reporters.

There was no evidence that Dole's affair in the late 1960s and early 1970s represented an ongoing or compulsive pattern of behavior. Dole had not made an issue of Democratic incumbent Bill Clinton's marital problems, although many of Dole's supporters had. Public statements acknowledging but not commenting on another news report are a flimsy basis for a news story. Those news organizations that initially decided not to report on past sexual activity and personal relationships that occurred many years earlier were correct and deserve higher marks. Some of the news organizations that eventually ran the Dole story gave it appropriately little play.

Dole's 1996 presidential campaign, his third bid for president, also gave reporters a chance to resurrect stories from previous campaigns about his financial dealings. One such story concerned his second wife Elizabeth's purchase of a Florida condominium from agriculture executive Dwayne Andreas, whose company benefited from her husband's actions in Congress. Reporters also reinvestigated the Doles' knowledge of business dealings involving a former fund-raiser who administered a blind trust for Elizabeth Dole and profited by some of the fund's activities.

While this topic was explored in Dole's earlier campaigns, all financial matters are fair game for scrutiny.

Mike Bowers: The Georgia state attorney general was the front-runner heading into the 1998 governor's race. Bowers, a Democrat-turned-Republican, had loyal support among state conservatives for his defense of state sex and marriage laws, including the successful defense of the state's sodomy laws before the U.S. Supreme Court. But Bowers's family-man image was shattered in 1997, shortly after he stepped down as attorney general to begin his campaign, when he held a press conference to confess a longtime extramarital relationship with a member of his state government staff. In April 1998, former secretary and ex-paramour Anne Davis granted an interview to *George* magazine, in which she revealed that Bowers provided ongoing financial support of $400 to $600 a month throughout their fifteen-year relationship. Bowers immediately ended the payments, which he said his wife had supported to help Davis with medical bills. Bowers resisted calls from some conservative and Republican leaders to drop out of the race for governor. He lost a July 1998 primary, although he ran stronger than expected, almost pushing his way into a runoff for the GOP nomination.

Bowers confessed publicly to his relationship with a member of his staff. In addition, the relationship clearly conflicted with Bowers's public position on state sex and marriage laws, which made adultery a crime. The issue was

also of concern to his conservative base, much of which abandoned his candidacy. Over-emphasis of the infidelity issue was the most significant blemish of the Georgia media's handling of this story.

Steve Henry: Kentucky lieutenant governor Steve Henry was preparing to launch his campaign for the Democratic Senate nomination in 1997, when his name emerged in a lawsuit involving a public employee with whom he had once had a consensual sexual relationship. A female county corrections officer testified in a sexual harassment lawsuit that she had had sex with Henry and another county official she also dated. The relationship was not related to the woman's claim that she and other female corrections officers were harassed on the job. In a story on the woman's testimony, the *Courier-Journal* newspaper in Louisville focused on her role negotiating a union contract with Jefferson County while Henry was a local commissioner. Henry said there was no link between the relationship and the county contract, which he had voted to approve.

While the relationship was between consenting adults, Henry's former role as a county official intersected with the woman's role as union negotiator. In addition, the relationship became part of an unrelated legal proceeding. Kentucky media deserve credit for not going overboard with this story throughout the primary campaign.

Raymond L. Flynn: As Democrat Ray Flynn was gearing up to run for Massachusetts governor in 1997, the *Boston Globe* published a lengthy story about the drinking habits of the former Boston mayor and U.S. ambassador to the Vatican. The *Globe* article suggested that Flynn understated both the frequency and the amount of his drinking, but said there was no indication that alcohol affected his public duties. The article also noted that, as mayor, Flynn frequently drank late into the night in Boston pubs, sometimes with *Globe* reporters and editors. The *Globe* decision to publish and document the long-standing rumors about Flynn's alcohol consumption sparked a journalistic debate that became the subject of a story on the CBS News show *60 Minutes*. Flynn accused the *Globe* of an anti–Irish Catholic bias. The former mayor ran for Congress instead of governor and lost in the Democratic primary.

The Globe *documented instances of ongoing private behavior, in this case heavy drinking, that was potentially debilitating. Other media, notably the rival* Boston Herald, *were critical of the coverage, noting that former Republican governor William Weld did not get the same scrutiny for incidents in which he appeared to be drunk in public. Perhaps he should have.*

Roy Romer: In 1990, during his first campaign for reelection, married Colorado governor Roy Romer denied a report in the alternative Denver newspaper *Westword* about a rumored romance with his top adviser, B. J. Thornberry. In his 1994 campaign for a third term, Romer denied the rumor again when his opponent accused the governor of using taxpayer money to pay for private phone calls to Thornberry. (By this time, she had taken a job in the Clinton administration in Washington.) Romer had already repaid the state for the bulk of the calls, saying the others were for official business. In 1998, after Romer decided to sit out that year's Senate race, the newsweekly magazine *Insight* did a story on Romer's relationship with his former aide. The *Insight* article was illustrated with images from a videotaped stakeout that showed Romer and the woman engaged in an extended kiss in an airport parking lot.

At the time, Romer was in his final term as governor and serving as chairman of the Democratic National Committee. This role put him in the position of responding publicly to the investigation of President Clinton's relationship with Monica Lewinsky. In an interview with the *Denver Post* and then at a lengthy press conference in Colorado, Romer confessed to a longstanding "affectionate"—but not "sexual"—extramarital relationship. Romer told reporters that he had been accurate in his earlier denials of the affair because the relationship was not sexual. Romer also said his family knew about and condoned his relationship with Thornberry.

Romer publicly admitted to a relationship with a former state employee that he previously told voters did not exist. The 1994 campaign accusation also required coverage. The 1990 Westword *article, while subsequently proved correct, was not well sourced or documented. More significant reporting on the relationship in 1990 and 1994 would have been appropriate.*

Bill Paxon: The U.S. representative from Buffalo, New York, was one of the leaders of the Republican revolution that took over Congress in 1994. He was also widely expected to mount a formidable challenge to House Majority Leader Richard Armey of Texas. But then came Paxon's surprise 1998 announcement that he would retire at the end of his term to spend more time with his family. Many reporters, as well as many of the forty-three-year-old congressman's House colleagues, doubted Paxon's stated reason for resigning. Soon reporters were investigating dark rumors on Capitol Hill that Paxon had resigned, possibly under pressure from a political enemy, to avoid the disclosure of an extramarital homosexual affair with a journalist who had committed suicide that same week. The rumor was false and completely unsubstantiated.

While many news reports and editorials about Paxon's retirement plans suggested there might be more to his announcement than family values, most news organizations that investigated the rumored relationship did not publish it. However, an editorial in an alternative newspaper in Paxon's New York district and discussions about the rumors on Buffalo-area talk radio programs prompted an angry, on-air denial from the congressman. The *Buffalo News* based an article on Paxon's denial, which was also mentioned in subsequent profiles of Paxon in various publications across the country.

 No evidence supported any published allegation.

Rudy Giuliani: Several New York City media outlets devoted teams of reporters, but very little ink or airtime, to finding information on Republican mayor Rudy Giuliani's marriage, including rumors that his wife planned to leave him. Reporters in New York also investigated Giuliani's long-denied relationship with communications director Cristyne F. Lategano. She was a controversial figure in the Giuliani administration who, gossip columns and reporters often noted, was once seen shopping for clothing with the mayor on East 57th Street. A 1995 article in

New York magazine suggested there was a relationship but offered no proof. In 1997, during the mayor's reelection campaign,
articles in the *Los Angeles Times* and *Vanity Fair* magazine took
the New York press to task for not reporting on widespread
rumors about the alleged difficulties in the Giuliani marriage.
Vanity Fair alleged that the Giuliani–Lategano rumor was true,
although reporting by the *New York Daily News* contradicted
key points in the magazine's story. Most news organizations
based their coverage of the *Vanity Fair* story on the mayor's on-
the-record denials. By the time Giuliani was reelected to a second term in 1997, no journalist had published credible information confirming any affair.

 *While investigating a rumored relationship
with a public employee is justifiable, no
evidence supported any published allegation.
Coverage based on public denials of unsubstantiated stories is unfair.*

David Beasley: In a 1996 gossip item, an alternative monthly
newspaper in Columbia, South Carolina, first published the
unproven rumors about Republican governor David Beasley's
alleged infidelity with his female communications director. The
State, the capital city's daily newspaper, also extensively investigated the rumor. Having decided that there was no evidence
to justify publishing a story about the rumors, the *State* shelved
its reporting on the matter. In late 1997, however, a political opponent of Beasley's began suggesting publicly that there might
be something to the widespread gossip about the governor. The
State responded with news stories explaining that the newspaper's reporting had disproved many of the rumors about the
governor and his marriage. South Carolina Democrats, however,
had plans to reintroduce the issue late in Beasley's struggling

campaign for a second term by quizzing him under oath about the relationship as part of a deposition in a Freedom of Information lawsuit. A *Time* magazine report on the Democrats' plans brought a strong denial from the governor, his pregnant wife, the former spokeswoman and alleged paramour, and her husband. The unusual joint news conference by the two couples made news across South Carolina and in other publications across the country.

No evidence supported any published allegation. Beasley's public denials and the on-the-record attacks by opponents required media explanations, and the Columbia State's proper handling of the story is exempted from this grade.

Mark Taylor: In 1998, Georgia lieutenant governor candidate Mark Taylor confirmed to reporters that he used illegal drugs while in his twenties. The *Macon Telegraph* asked Taylor about his drug use after a source sent the newspaper copies of his sealed deposition from a 1992 custody fight, in which he admitted under oath to using marijuana and cocaine. Taylor's opponents tried to make an issue of his drug use, which the state senator said ended fifteen years earlier, after he learned that his wife was pregnant. Despite his rival's snipes—and a brutal, unsubstantiated television advertisement that suggested he had an ongoing narcotics problem—Taylor prevailed in the Democratic primary, a runoff vote, and the general election that fall.

Taylor's adult drug use ended years before. Taylor also admitted to his drug use in a legal proceeding, albeit in a sealed court document leaked to a newspaper. Criticism

and attacks by Taylor's political opponents
guaranteed ongoing coverage of the issue.

Henry B. Gonzalez: After thirty-seven years in Congress, former House Banking Committee chairman Henry Gonzalez spent more than half of his final two-year term at home in Texas recovering from a heart ailment. The Texas media took little notice of the Democrat's extended absence until a July 1998 story in the *Houston Chronicle*—almost a year after Gonzalez cast his last vote in the House. But even then few were willing to comment on the record about the legendary lawmaker's decision to stay in office rather than retire before the end of the term, as he originally promised. Gonzalez returned to work two months later—fourteen months after he'd left and shortly before his son won the campaign to succeed him.

Gonzalez's health clearly affected his performance in office, since he was not actually in Washington to represent his constituents for more than half of his term. The congressman's absence deserved more scrutiny than it received from his home state press, despite his venerable position as one of the longest-serving members of Congress.

Dan Burton, Helen Chenoweth, Henry Hyde and Bob Livingston: The sex lives of each of these four Republican congressmen who ran for office as "family values" candidates made news during the thirteen-month investigation, impeachment and Senate trial of President Clinton. Dan Burton once generated national headlines by calling the president a "scumbag." While Burton's remark focused on Clinton's money-raising practices in the 1996 campaign, an alternative newspaper in Indianapolis used the remark to raise questions about Burton's personal conduct as a state legislator and congressman. In September 1998, Burton preempted additional news reports about his past by telling his constituents about an illegitimate child that he fathered in the 1980s in an extramarital relationship with a state employee. *Vanity Fair* magazine canceled an expected profile after Burton's admission, but the writer later published additional allegations and rumors of sexual misconduct in the online magazine *Salon*. Follow-up reporting by other news organizations focused on Burton's financial relationship with one of the women that *Salon* named, not the personal relationship.

Burton's relationship and child with a state employee deserved scrutiny. Burton's pre-emptive announcement guaranteed coverage. Other women linked to Burton by Salon *also had professional connections, although without a public confession from the congressman these stories required significant substantiating evidence and sourcing to be newsworthy.*

Also in September 1998, the *Idaho Statesman* ran a story about Representative Chenoweth's relationship with a married business partner before her election to Congress, while she was single in the mid-1980s. The newspaper decided to report on Chenoweth's long-rumored romance after she released a series of television campaign ads critical of Clinton's character and conduct. The *Spokane Spokesman-Review* also reported that Chenoweth had lied to one of its reporters about the relationship when asked about it in an unpublished interview in a previous campaign. Chenoweth said she did not recall the interview.

While past relationships ordinarily are not newsworthy, Chenoweth's outspoken positions on "family values" and Clinton's behavior invited scrutiny. That the relationship involved a business partner didn't help her case.

Judiciary Committee chairman Henry Hyde, who presided over the House impeachment hearings, admitted to an extramarital relationship with a married woman in the 1960s, before he was elected to Congress. News of this affair was also unearthed by *Salon*, which learned about the relationship from a Florida retiree who was a friend of the woman's former husband.

 Hyde's focus on the legal aspects of the Monica Lewinsky case shielded the Judiciary Committee chairman from the hypocrisy charges leveled against Chenoweth, whose criticism of Clinton emphasized character. Past affairs, especially those that do not involve a professional relationship, are not newsworthy, although Hyde's admission to Salon *gave other news organizations a peg for their stories. Hyde's defenders' unfounded accusations that the White House masterminded the* Salon *story produced more coverage of the issue than it otherwise might have received.*

Bob Livingston's extramarital relationships were uncovered by *Hustler* magazine publisher Larry Flynt, the pornographer who took out a full-page advertisement in the *Washington Post* offering money to anyone who could offer proof of such affairs. Days before the House impeachment vote in December 1998, Speaker-designate Livingston told the Republican caucus about his past. Then, in a dramatic floor speech on the day of the vote, Livingston stunned his colleagues once again, announcing that he would resign and challenging President Clinton to do the same.

 Preemptive disclosures by their very nature are public statements that are legitimate news stories. Out of respect for Livingston's family, subsequent coverage of his admitted affairs did not delve into the details of the relationships.

Newt Gingrich:

Many profiles of House Speaker Newt Gingrich discussed the breakup of his first marriage in the 1980s, including allegations of infidelity that he had addressed in interviews long before the GOP took control of Congress in 1994. However, few journalists paid attention to rumored dalliances during the Speaker's second marriage, even during the House impeachment debate and amid revelations about affairs involving his colleagues. In the summer of 1999, after he stepped down as Speaker and left Congress, Gingrich filed for divorce. A short time later, the *Star* supermarket tabloid published a report alleging a long-standing affair between the fifty-six-year-old former congressman and a thirty-three-year-old congressional aide. The woman was previously identified in a long 1995 *Vanity Fair* profile of Gingrich as his "favorite breakfast companion." She was also described but not named in pornographer Larry Flynt's *Flynt Report*, a glossy publication summarizing various rumors about Clinton's congressional critics. Lawyers for Gingrich's wife won a court fight to depose the congressional staff member about the relationship before the former Speaker agreed to terms for divorce and the deposition was canceled.

The press flunked on this case for showing too much discretion. The divorces and marriages of private citizens, such as Gingrich, are not generally newsworthy. However, the House Speaker's extramarital affair with a member of a congressional committee staff while he was in office should have raised ethical questions. At the same time, conducting such an affair during a criminal investigation and sex scandal involving the president of the United States is potentially reckless behavior that Capitol Hill reporters should have investigated.

George W. Bush: "When I was young and irresponsible I was young and irresponsible," the Republican governor of Texas and the son of the former president told *Newsweek* in 1998. Bush's statement about drinking and illegal drug use raised more questions about his background than it answered. The result was the widespread publication and broadcast of numerous unsubstantiated rumors during the early part of his White House bid. Bush told reporters in 1999 that he would have been able to pass a security clearance test based on drug questions any time during his father's administration. That constituted an effective denial of illegal drug use since 1974, when Bush was in his late twenties. Bush also spoke to many reporters about his decision to give up drinking after his fortieth birthday.

Youthful alcohol abuse and experimentation with drugs do not usually deserve the extensive scrutiny Bush's background received during the initial stages of the 2000 presidential race. Repetition of specific but unproven rumors about Bush's alleged drug use were completely unjustified without significant comment on the validity of the story. However, Bush's admitted alcohol abuse extended well into his adult years, as did the period about which he would not answer questions about drug use. Bush's own on-the-record statements on the topic also invited investigation. And his tough policies on juvenile crime raised questions about Bush's own behavior during the period in which he was "young and irresponsible."

One completely unsubstantiated story about Bush involved an alleged photograph of the future governor during his college years, showing him drunk and dancing naked on a bar. The story was first reported in the *Star*, the same supermarket tabloid that first published the Gennifer Flowers story. Some news organizations ran items quoting Bush after he told *Texas Monthly* that he did not think any such photo ever existed. Nonetheless, the rumored picture continued to be the subject of late-night comedy TV monologues. The unseen photograph was also described in some mainstream press accounts, including the *Wall Street Journal* and the *Washington Post*.

 No evidence supported any published account of the photograph.

Kirk Fordice: Republican Kirk Fordice was elected governor of Mississippi in 1991 with strong backing from the state's influential Christian conservatives. In 1993, he stunned supporters by announcing that he and his wife planned to divorce. The announcement was not just news to the state but to Fordice's wife, who issued her own public statement contradicting the governor on their plans to separate. The couple then issued a joint press release saying they were working to salvage their marriage. In 1996, one year into the governor's second term, Fordice was nearly killed when he overturned his Jeep returning to the state capital from a private lunch date with his former high school sweetheart in Tennessee. News reports at the time said Fordice was seen with a woman other than his wife in a restaurant, holding hands and drinking wine before the accident. Police said alcohol was not a factor in the car wreck. In June 1999, a TV reporter snapped a picture of Fordice and his recently widowed girlfriend as the couple exited a plane together returning from a French vacation. Shortly after Fordice's overseas trip with the woman, the governor once again announced plans to divorce.

The privacy the press might ordinarily afford a discreet, nonprofessional relationship was offset by Fordice's vocal stance on "family values," his public statements about his marriage and the Mississippi public's right to know the circumstances surrounding a mysterious car accident that hospitalized the state's governor for several months.

John and Cindy McCain: Aspiring first lady Cindy McCain and her husband, Republican senator John McCain of Arizona, preempted intrusive media inquiries about her two-year addiction to prescription painkillers by granting an exclusive interview on the subject to NBC *Dateline*. The interview aired in October 1999, just before much of the general public began focusing on the presidential nominating process. NBC's exclusive was news to a national audience, but not to voters in the McCains' home state. In 1994, local reporters grilled the McCains and federal prosecutors about whether the senator's wife received special treatment when she was allowed to apply for a diversion program rather than face prosecution for stealing painkillers from an international medical charity she headed. As with the 1999 interview, the McCains preempted damaging news reports by granting a series of interviews to selected Arizona news organizations, but none from the *Arizona Republic*. A cartoon in that newspaper portrayed Cindy McCain holding a third-world child upside down, trying to shake out drugs to feed her habit.

Legal matters involving the candidate's family are newsworthy. The McCains also raised the issue with the press in on-the-record interviews.

John McCain's private past was also the subject of some press scrutiny. Many profiles of the presidential candidate made reference to infidelities during the senator's first marriage, which he discussed in interviews for a 1995 book about the Vietnam War's effects on five prominent Naval Academy graduates. McCain took full responsibility for his role in the divorce.

Past affairs are not generally newsworthy, although McCain first put the topic on the record. Most news organizations reported on the issue in context in extended profiles and interviews with the candidate.

Exhibit B

In Their Own Defense

Readers and viewers rarely appreciate just how much most journalists anguish over decisions to publish damaging or embarrassing details about a politician's personal behavior. But front-page headlines and the stories below them usually do not convey that difficult decision-making process. Occasionally, an editor or reporter will write an editorial or an extended editor's note that describes this process. These stories can clarify a news organization's motives and values. They also help readers and viewers put stories in the context in which the news organization intended. The following three articles are examples of this kind of writing.

GETTING THE PACKWOOD STORY

This article by Washington Post *executive editor Leonard Downie Jr. explains his decision to publish allegations of sexual misconduct by Senator Bob Packwood. Downie's article was published on November 29, 1992, a week after the* Post's *first Packwood story.*

Few decisions are as difficult to make in our newsroom as when to publish a story based on investigative reporting that could affect the reputation of an individual or an institution or, in some cases, could alter the course of events. The decision is made more difficult when we are assembling information that previously has been hidden from public view. Is our reporting complete enough? Is there something important we still don't know? Do we sufficiently understand the pattern and meaning of the facts we have pieced together? Is the story we propose to publish sufficiently full, accurate and fair?

These are the questions we reviewed for weeks until the publication on Sunday, Nov. 22, of the story detailing the uninvited sexual advances Sen. Bob Packwood has made to women who have worked for him or with him. The story was based on interviews with former staff members and lobbyists, including 10 women who, independently of one another, agreed to give us specific accounts of Packwood's behavior toward them. The story was the culmination of investigative reporting by the *Washington Post* that had begun in early October and continued until—and even during—the day before the story appeared in the newspaper.

Because this process is not observed by our readers, the decision about when such a story is ready to publish, and in what form, can appear to be arbitrary or determined by unseen events or pressures. In the case of the story about Packwood, some readers have asked why it was not published before the November 3 election, in which Packwood, a 60-year-old Oregon Republican, narrowly won reelection to a fifth term in the U.S. Senate.

The answer is that on Election Day we still needed to do much more reporting, writing and editing before we had a story sufficiently full, accurate and fair to publish. We wanted to publish as quickly as possible but not before the story was truly ready. As it turned out, our work could not be completed until three weeks after the election. Publication was possible then only because of extraordinarily productive work by a team of reporters and editors working long hours.

A freelance writer, Florence Graves, first contacted the *Post* in September with information about Packwood that she had gathered while reporting for another publication about sexual harassment on Capitol Hill in the wake of the Clarence Thomas hearings. She was hired on a contract basis to work with *Post* staff members, including reporter Charles Shepard, beginning early in October. When first approached by the *Post*, those who said Packwood had made sexual advances to them were reluctant to talk about their experiences on the record for a newspaper article.

By late October, the reporting had progressed far enough to question Packwood about accounts of six women who agreed to be named in interviews with him. *Post* reporters asked to interview the senator on October 23, but Packwood did not agree to be interviewed until the 29th. In that conversation Packwood denied making sexual advances toward any of the women. He asked for time to review his office records and gather any information that might "tend to detract from the credibility" of the women identified to him.

Beginning on October 31, Packwood sent the *Post* eight statements about three of the women from people who knew them, including people who worked for Packwood. None dealt directly with the women's accounts of sexual advances by Packwood; instead, some of them suggested that several of the women may have been attracted to Packwood, might have invited his advances or were untruthful.

At this time, Packwood also asked editors of the *Post* for an opportunity, when any story was ready to be published, to prepare a statement from him for such a story.

With the November 3 election approaching, the reporters working on the story and their editors reviewed in detail the information that had been gathered thus far. They concluded that there were still too many loose ends, and too much work left to do, to publish a story before the election. Packwood was informed that the *Post*'s reporting would continue.

The story published on November 22 contained or made reference to much significant information that was gathered during November in dozens more interviews, including several conversations with Packwood. This additional information included accounts from another woman who said Packwood had made unwelcome sexual advances, as well as further corroboration of many of the women's accounts by people these women talked to after the incidents occurred.

The *Post* also acquired more information from former Packwood employees about how his behavior created an undercurrent of tension and resentment within his office over a period of years. And there were accounts of how the statements sent to the *Post* about the personal lives of some of the women had become a source of contention among Packwood's friends and former aides, who said they counseled him to acknowledge his behavior rather than appear to be smearing the reputations of the women.

The story also quoted a statement of apology by Packwood, which he sent to the *Post* on Friday, November 20, after being informed that the story would be published the following Sunday. It was. By then, after another long day of editing, it was ready.

A SUMMER SPENT INVESTIGATING INTANGIBLE ALLEGATIONS

This article by editorial writer Cindi Ross Scoppe appeared in the State, *South Carolina's capital city newspaper. Scoppe's story was published October 1, 1998, days after* Time *magazine pub-*

lished a story about rumors spread by state Democrats that then-governor David Beasley, a Republican waging a losing fight for a second term, was involved in an extramarital affair with his former communications director.

These are the new political rules: Think up the most horrible rumors you can about your opponent and then start spreading them. No evidence? No problem.

We've all heard the one about Mary Wood Beasley barging past the SLED [security] agents guarding David Beasley's office and catching her husband in the act with communications director Ginny Wolfe.

But did you hear that Marilyn Monroe is alive and [state House Minority Leader] Jim Hodges has been dating her?

OK, so that's not a good comparison. That one has not been investigated and found totally lacking in either credibility or even evidence.

The Beasley-Wolfe rumors, by contrast, were investigated. Exhaustively.

In the summer of 1996, I spent two months on that assignment. (Reporters at other news organizations did, too.) I solicited allegations. I begged my sources to put me in touch with their sources. I found two things: Every rumor that included a specific place or date or other element that could be verified failed to check out. And original sources—or even my sources' sources—were never available.

The phone calls started in early July, after a local alternative publication reported the rumor. In the first wave, every reporter I know was inundated with rumors that the first lady had packed up the couple's three children and flown home to her parents in Alabama over the alleged affair.

Callers were insistent. They were angry when I told them that I had checked, that Mary Wood Beasley was still at the governor's mansion on the day the rumors had her leaving, and for several days afterward. They were angry when I told them Mrs. Beasley was actually attending a National Governors Association meeting in Puerto Rico with her husband, with lots of witnesses, while she was supposed to have been fleeing home to daddy.

I called the governor's mansion and talked at length with Mrs. Beasley about the allegations on one of the days that political junkies, as well as ordinary people, were insisting she was in Alabama. She denied that she had ever left her husband or that the marriage was anything other than happy. A loyal, long-time Democrat told me about intimate dinners he and his wife had with a blissful first couple.

As the weeks went by, Mrs. Beasley's presence in Columbia did nothing to deter the rumors. If anything, they intensified, and they became more bizarre and more specific. Callers insisted that Mrs. Wolfe's husband, George, had filed divorce papers in Richland County. (Not true; we checked.)

A set of frantic phone calls to the newspaper one Friday afternoon had Gov. Beasley and Mrs. Wolfe walking out of the governor's office together, dressed in shorts, for a long weekend. I checked. Both were at their desks.

My favorite rumor—which didn't even involve Mrs. Wolfe—was an explanation of why the governor had fired Boykin Rose as director of public safety: There was a dispute over their wife-swapping arrangement. I have to admit my investigation into that one was rather cursory.

I had just about concluded that there was nothing else to do—short of tailing the governor day and night—when an editor at the newspaper told me about a conversation he had over the weekend with a longtime friend. The friend recounted having lunch with two of her friends and one of her friends' friends,

Mary Wood Beasley. Mrs. Beasley, obviously oblivious to the presence of someone she had never met before, supposedly spent the entire time unloading about her husband's infidelity.

I was sickened and excited at the same time. How do I contact your friend, I asked the editor. He wasn't sure she'd talk but promised to check. And so for what seemed like weeks, we negotiated back and forth. I backed off my insistence that she talk on the record. No luck. I backed off a face-to-face interview. No luck. Backed off even knowing her name. Still no luck. I wouldn't even call her; she could call me. Still nothing.

Finally, in desperation, I promised I would never write a word of what she told me. I simply needed to know—so I could decide whether to keep digging—if there was one person out there who actually had some second-hand knowledge. And still I never heard from my mystery diner.

But none of that matters now. The Starring of politics has come to South Carolina. (For the record, I think the Paula Jones lawsuit was an outrageous abuse of our judicial system, that the Supreme Court erred terribly in letting it go forward and that Ken Starr desperately needs to get a life.) With its own ridiculous lawsuit, the Democratic Party subpoenaed Gov. Beasley and then used that subpoena (which has since been dropped) as a way to revive these discredited rumors. Rumors that every politician in the state knows have no credible basis.

Fortunately, reporters have done the work and are able (when they are willing) to tell the public there's no basis for the allegations. This time.

Will the next slandered politician be so lucky?

A TOUGH DECISION

Karen Baker, editor of the Idaho Statesman, *published this editorial September 15, 1998, about why her newspaper published a story about Representative Helen Chenoweth's relationship with a married man in the 1980s, before she was elected to Congress.*

Wednesday was not an easy day to be an editor at the *Idaho Statesman*. It was likely not an easy day to be U.S. Rep. Helen Chenoweth, either.

The *Statesman*'s decision to break the story in which Chenoweth said she regretted a previous personal relationship with a married man did not come easily, and made all of us involved uncomfortable.

The only reason, and I cannot emphasize that word enough, that we published the story was that Chenoweth made "personal conduct and integrity" an issue in her recent TV advertisements. Just as we frequently do with our popular AdWatch features, we held her accountable for her claims.

Reporters and editors routinely hear rumors about news makers and, in particular, candidates for office. Many of them we do not even bother to try to check out, because there is no public issue involved.

That had been the case with previous reports about the congressman, too, which reporters have heard for several years. The "stories" about her conduct that we had heard did not matter, and were not relevant.

When she made "personal conduct and integrity" an issue in her ads, however, we believed it was our responsibility to challenge her and to determine whether she had lived up to the standards she was espousing.

We decided to print the story only after a series of conversations with editors, reporters and the publisher. We weighed the possible consequences of publishing and not publishing, and considered the pain the story would cause those individuals involved. The scales tipped in favor of going with the story.

Still, we took great care in choosing our words when writing the story. Unlike other media, we did not use words like "confessed" or "admitted," but rather played it straight with the verb "said." We did not try to characterize the relationship in any way.

And because the ads alone precipitated the story, we were careful to focus the story on the ads. We intentionally did not mention Larry LaRocco, who opposed Chenoweth in 1994 and whose extramarital relationship likely cost him the election.

We discussed where to play the story in the paper, and decided that, while it was a Page 1 story, it did not belong at the top of the page.

So there was no attempt to play up the story to sell newspapers. The story was not visible in the newsrack; it was at the bottom of the page. We deliberated over the headline, again choosing our words carefully.

None of us involved in the decision was eager to publish; we are all uncomfortable reporting on anyone's personal life, and under normal circumstances we would not. Congressman Chenoweth, however, made her conduct a public issue. Had there been no TV spots, there would have been no story.

I, for one, wish the commercials had never aired.

Notes

PROLOGUE

1. Rudolph W. Giuliani, interview by Larry King, *Larry King Live*, CNN, August 26, 1997; Michael Sponhour, "'I've Been Faithful,' Governor Vows," *Columbia* (South Carolina) *State*, September 30, 1998, A1.

2. "Loose Lips," *The Point* (Columbia, South Carolina), June 1996, online archive (http://www.mindspring.com/~scpoint/point/9606/lips.html); Cindi Ross Scoppe, "Media Found No Facts in Beasley Rumors," *Columbia* (South Carolina) *State*, August 6, 1997, A9; Adam Zagorin, "Catching the Starr Bug," *Time*, October 5, 1998, 33; Howard Kurtz, "A Tale to Wag a Thousand Tongues," *Washington Post*, October 5, 1998, D1.

3. *Washington Post*–ABC News polling data based on random telephone interviews with 1,285 adults from December 19–20, 1998 (http://www.washingtonpost.com/wp-srv/politics/polls/polls.htm); Pew polling data based on a Princeton Survey Research Associates telephone survey of 1,203 adults February 18–21, 1999 (http://www.people-press.org/feb99que.htm).

4. Pew polling data based on a Princeton Survey Research Associates telephone survey of 1,205 adults September 1–12, 1999 (http://www.people-press.org/sept99rpt.htm).

5. Princeton Survey, September 1–12, 1999.

6. "Address to the Nation on Testimony before the Independent Counsel's Grand Jury," *Weekly Compilation of Presidential Documents* 34, no. 34 (August 21, 1998), 1637–1647. Retrieved online from GPO Access (http://www.access.gpo.gov, DOCID:pd24au98_txt-4).

CHAPTER 1

1. Walter Isaacson, e-mail message to authors, November 5, 1999.

2. Leonard Downie Jr., interview with authors, November 9, 1999.

3. Morton M. Kondracke, interview with authors, June 28, 1999.

4. Pew polling data based on a Princeton Survey Research Associates telephone survey of 1,205 adults September 1–12, 1999. (http://www.people-press.org/sept99rpt.htm).

5. Larry J. Sabato, *Feeding Frenzy: How Attack Journalism Has Transformed American Politics* (New York: Free Press, 1991).

6. For explanations of Bush's role in both deals, see George Lardner Jr., "A Baseless Suspicion," *Washington Post*, July 30, 1999, A20; and Lois Romano and George Lardner Jr., "RBI: Revenue Brought In," *Washington Post*, July 31, 1999, A12.

7. Larry J. Sabato and S. Robert Lichter, *When Should the Watchdogs Bark? Media Coverage of the Clinton Scandals* (Washington, D.C.: Center for Media and Public Affairs, 1994), 15–28.

8. Charles R. Babcock, "Candidate of Humble Origins Is Now Well-Off," *Washington Post*, November 3, 1996, A38; Phil Kuntz, "Perfectly Legal," *Wall Street Journal*, October 10, 1996, A1; *Nightline*, ABC News, August 20, 1996; Sara Fritz, "Dole's Own McDougal," *Los Angeles Times*, August 7, 1996, A5.

9. Greg McDonald, "Gonzalez AWOL from Congress for Almost a Year," *Houston Chronicle*, July 5, 1998, 1; Michelle Mittelstadt, "Gonzalez Back at Capital to Complete His Last Term," *Austin American-Statesman*, September 14, 1998, A2.

10. Neil Mclaughlin, "Can't Be Forced to Resign," *Los Angeles Times*, August 10, 1986, 14; Donald M. Rothberg, "Illness, Age Can Signal End of Political Career," Associated Press, April 20, 1991; "Tejeda Receives Approval to Take Oath in Ceremony Here," *San Antonio Express-News*, January 8, 1997, 12A; Cindy Tumiel, "Tejeda Puts Off Return to D.C.," *San Antonio Express-News*, January 30, 1997, 1A; "Rep. Frank Tejeda Dies of Brain Cancer at 51," *Washington Post*, January 31, 1997, A6.

11. Christopher B. Daly, "Tsongas Confirms His Abdominal Cancer, Says He Still Aspires to the Presidency," *Washington Post*, December 1, 1992, A4; Walter Berns, editor, *After the People Vote:*

A Guide to the Electoral College, rev. and enlarged edition (Washington, D.C.: The AEI Press, 1992), 25–29.

12. Joseph Neff, "Funderburk Pleads No Contest," *Raleigh News & Observer,* October 31, 1995, A1; "Commercial Politics: Etheridge Attacks Funderburk on Car Wreck," *Raleigh News & Observer,* October 19, 1996, A3.

13. John E. Yang, "Rough-and-Tumble Hill Debate," *Washington Post,* November 18, 1995, A22; Spencer S. Hsu, "Police Called to Moran's Home," *Washington Post,* June 24, 1999, B7; Spencer S. Hsu and Patricia Davis, "After Call for Help, Moran's Wife Seeks Divorce," *Washington Post,* June 25, 1999, B1; Stephen Dinan, "Moran's Spouse Files for Divorce," *Washington Times,* June 25, 1999, C3; Spencer S. Hsu, "Rep. Moran Claims Wife Sought to Humiliate Him," *Washington Post,* July 16, 1999, B7; Spencer S. Hsu, "Moran's Woes Financial as Well as Marital," *Washington Post,* August 3, 1999, B1.

14. Krista Reese, "The Lights Went Out in Georgia," *George* (May 1998): 70; Kathey Pruitt, "Bowers Still Helping Her, Alleged Mistress Says," *Atlanta Journal and Constitution,* April 14, 1998, B3; Kathey Pruitt, "Bowers Says He Aided Ex-lover Out of Charity," *Atlanta Journal and Constitution,* April 15, 1998, E2; Kathey Pruitt, "Bowers Says He Stopped Payments to Ex-Mistress," *Atlanta Journal and Constitution,* April 17, 1998, B3; Kathey Pruitt and Charmagne Helton, "Bowers' Ex-lover Talks to Local Media," *Atlanta Journal and Constitution,* April 30, 1998, D3.

15. Douglas Feiden,"Rudy Marriage on Rocks—Mag 'Intimate' Relations with Top Aide Alleged," *New York Daily News,* August 4, 1997, 5; Lee Bandy, "Beasley Foe Rides Rumors Into '98 Battle," *Columbia* (South Carolina) *State,* August 6, 1997, A1; Brian Weber, "Romer: Rumors Untrue," *Colorado Springs Gazette Telegraph,* June 7, 1990, A1; "Some Excerpts," *Denver Post,* February 7, 1998, A11.

16. Rick McDonough, "Henry Dated Corrections Officer During Contract Talks," *Louisville Courier-Journal,* July 16, 1997, 1B; Al Cross, "Baesler Criticizes Henry's Relationship," *Louisville Courier-Journal,* July 19, 1997, 16. 1B.

17. "Personalities," *Washington Post,* July 7, 1990, C3; Heidi Mae Bratt, "Undaunted, Conyers Makes 2nd Run for Mayor," *Detroit News,* August 24, 1993, 1; Jessica Lee, "Watergate Attacker to Defend Clinton," *USA Today,* December 18, 1998, 22A.

18. Gail Sheehy, "The Inner Quest of Newt Gingrich," *Vanity Fair* (September 1995): at 220; Martin Fletcher, "Gingrich Wife Rules Out Bid for White House," *Times* (London), August 10, 1995; Margaret Carlson, "Newt's Bad Old Days," *Time* (August 21, 1995): 31; Stephen Talbot, "Newt's Glass House," *Salon* (August 28, 1998): http://www.salon.com/news/1998/08/28news.html; "Newt Gingrich: Devalued Moral Values," *Flynt Report* 1 (1999): 40–41; Richard Gooding, "Newt's New Love," *Star* (August 24, 1999): 10; Patricia J. Mays, "Lawyers for Gingrich's Wife Plan Deposition of Woman," *Atlanta Journal*, August 13, 1999, A9.

19. "Key Events in Packwood Case," *Washington Post*, September 8, 1995, A17; Helen Dewar and Florence Graves, "Packwood: Behavior Was 'Wrong,'" *Washington Post*, December 11, 1992, A1; Florence Graves and Charles E. Shepard, "Packwood Accused of Sexual Advances," *Washington Post*, November 22, 1992, A1.

20. Howard Kurtz, "A Long-Simmering Story Explodes Into the Mainstream," *Washington Post*, February 20, 1999, A9; Howard Kurtz, "NBC Ready to Air 'Jane Doe' Interview," *Washington Post*, February 24, C1. For background and complete coverage of the accusations against President Clinton, see the "Clinton Accused" special report on washingtonpost.com: http://www.washingtonpost.com/wp-srv/politics/special/clinton/clinton.htm.)

21. Helen Dewar and David S. Broder, "Packwood, Under Siege, Tells Senate He'll Quit," *Washington Post*, September 8, 1995, A1.

22. Dee Lane, Steve Mayes, and James Long, "Bob Packwood: Power, Money and Alcohol," *Portland Oregonian*, January 17, 1993, A1.

23. "Packwood: Drinking Erased Memory," *Washington Post*, August 30, 1995, A9.

24. Sabato, *Feeding Frenzy*, 31–33, 47.

25. Walter Robinson, "Flynn at the Vatican: His Mayoral Style Didn't Cut It," *Boston Globe*, October 3, 1997, A1; Scot Lehigh, "Of Alcohol, Politicians, and What Makes a News Story," *Boston Globe*, October 3, 1997, A15; Kelly Heyboer, "Blasted in Boston," *American Journalism Review* (December 1, 1997): 10; *60 Minutes*, CBS, April 12, 1998.

26. Jack Thomas, "Flynn Furor," *Boston Globe*, October 20, 1997, A15.

27. Scot Lehigh, "Poll Data Support Reporting on Flynn," *Boston Globe*, November 2, 1997, A22.

28. Howard Fineman with Mark Hosenball, "The Bush Brothers," *Newsweek* (November 2, 1998): 30; Dan Balz, "Bush Goes Further on Question of Drugs," *Washington Post*, August 20, 1999, A1; Stephen Barr and Ben White, "Agencies Vary in Handling Drug Issue," *Washington Post*, August 23, 1999, A15.

29. Stephen Barr and Ben White, "Agencies Vary in Handling Drug Issue," *Washington Post*, August 23, 1999, A15.

30. Barr and White, "Agencies Vary"; Standard Form 86, "Questionnaire for National Security Positions," U.S. Office of Personnel Management, revised September 1995.

31. Lance Wallace, "Taylor Addresses Anonymous Reports on Drugs," *Macon Telegraph*, April 14, 1998, B2; Peter Mantius, "Democratic Hopeful's Past Drug Use Surfaces," *Atlanta Journal and Constitution*, April 15, 1998, E2; "Election '98 Adwatch," *Atlanta Journal and Constitution*, October 17, 1998, F2.

32. Larry J. Sabato and S. Robert Lichter, *When Should the Watchdogs Bark? Media Coverage of the Clinton Scandals* (Washington, D.C.: Center for Media and Public Affairs, 1994), 9–19, 15–28, 65–71.

33. Jennifer Gavin and Adriel Bettelheim, "Benson: Taxpayers Foot Calls by Romer," *Denver Post*, November 3, 1994, B1; Katie Kerwin, "Romer Phone Calls Questioned," *Rocky Mountain News*, November 3, 1994, 5A; Fred Brown, "Politicos Decry Voter Cynicism but Are Happy to Exploit It," *Denver Post*, November 4, 1994, B1.

34. Dick Polman and Steve Goldstein, "Powell Looks More Like a Candidate," *Philadelphia Inquirer*, October 22, 1995, A1; Howard Fineman, Eleanor Clift, and Evan Thomas, "Powell on the Brink," *Newsweek* (November 6, 1995): 36.

35. Leonard Downie Jr., interview with authors, November 9, 1999.

36. "Vice President's Daughter Cited for Having a Beer in Her Hands," Associated Press, September 30, 1995; Martin Weil, "Gore's Daughter Cited for Alcohol Possession," *Washington Post*, October 1, 1995, B1; "Gores Keep Citation a Family Matter," *Washington Times*, October 2, 1995, C5; *Morning News*, Fox, October 3, 1995.

37. Morton M. Kondracke, interview with authors, June 28, 1999.

38. Larry Van Dyne, "Paradise Lost," *Washingtonian* (January 1998): 73.

39. Ann McDaniel, interview with authors, July 23, 1999.

40. M. L. Stein, "First Daughter Goes to College," *Editor & Publisher* (October 4, 1997): 12; James N. Thurman, "Debut of 'the Boyfriend' Erodes Media Pact to Respect Privacy," *Christian Science Monitor*, May 6, 1998, 3; Kate Coyne, "Chelsea Mourning Break-up: Friends," *New York Post*, November 25, 1998, 3; Howard Kurtz, "Open Season on Chelsea," *Washington Post*, November 26, 1998, C1; Elizabeth Shogren, "White House Tried to Block Chelsea Article," *Los Angeles Times*, February 5, 1999, A19; Howard Kurtz, "*People* Magazine Goes Ahead with Article on Chelsea," *Washington Post*, February 5, 1999, C2; Jennifer Bojorquez, "Chelsea Clinton Fodder Yet for the Mainstream Media?" *Sacramento Bee*, February 8, 1999, C1; Landon Y. Jones, "Road Warriors," *People* (July 20, 1992): 68.

41. Mandy Grunwald, 1993 interview with Mark Stencel; see Larry King with Mark Stencel, *On the Line: The New Road to the White House* (New York: Harcourt Brace, 1993), 141.

42. Steve Meissner, "McCain's Wife Says She Has Drug Problem," *Arizona Daily Star*, August 22, 1994, 1A; John Kolbe, "'I'm Cindy, and I'm an Addict,'" *Phoenix Gazette*, August 22, 1994, B5; Martin Van Der Werf and Susan Leonard, "McCain's Wife Likely Won't Be Prosecuted," *Arizona Republic*, August 23, 1994, A1; "The Senator's Wife," *Arizona Daily Star*, August 24, 1994, 14A.

43. "Clinton Accused" special report on washingtonpost.com: http://www.washingtonpost.com/wp-srv/politics/special/clinton/clinton.htm).

44. Robert Timberg, *The Nightingale's Song* (New York: Touchstone, 1996), 239; *CNN Late Edition*, CNN, March 2, 1999; *Sunday Morning*, CBS, April 18, 1999; *60 Minutes*, CBS, June 6, 1999; *20/20*, ABC, September 8, 1999.

45. Kevin Merida, "Dole's 'Emergency Divorce,'" *Washington Post*, August 7, 1996, A1; Blaine Harden, "A Seething Dole Intensifies Attack," *Washington Post*, October 26, 1996, A1; Howard Kurtz, "A Big Story—but Only Behind the Scenes," *Washington Post*, November 13, 1996, D1.

46. David Brock, "The Strange Odyssey of Michael Huffington," *Esquire*, January 1999, retrieved from Dow Jones Interactive.

47. Joe Salkowski, "Nearly Outed, Kolbe Confirms That He's Gay," *Arizona Daily Star*, August 2, 1996, 1A; "Kolbe Wins Seventh Straight Term," *Arizona Daily Star*, November 6, 1996, 9A.

48. James Bradshaw, "Ruccia Questions Kasich Aide's Setup,"

Columbus Dispatch, September 13, 1996, 6B; Sabrina Eaton, "Opponent Challenges Kasich on Financial Ties to Chief Aide," *Cleveland Plain Dealer*, September 13, 1996, 23A; "Out of Bounds: Ruccia's Attack on Kasich Is Deplorable," *Columbus Dispatch*, September 24, 1996, 8A; Karen Tumulty, "The Baiting Game," *Time*, October 14, 1996, 61; Annie Groer and Ann Gerhart, "The Reliable Source," *Washington Post*, December 12, 1996, C3; Joe Hallett, Roger K. Lowe, and Jonathan Riskind, "In His Politics and in His Heart, Kasich Is Never Far From Home," *Columbus Dispatch*, June 6, 1999, 1A.

49. Lois Romano and George Lardner Jr., "1986: A Life-Changing Year," *Washington Post*, July 25, 1999, A1.

50. Sabato, *Feeding Frenzy*, 18, 20, 117–118.

CHAPTER 2

1. Morton M. Kondracke, interview with authors, June 28, 1999.

2. *This Week*, ABC News, January 18, 1998.

3. Ann McDaniel, interview with authors, July 23, 1999.

4. Larry J. Sabato, *Feeding Frenzy: How Attack Journalism Has Transformed American Politics* (New York: Free Press, 1991), 55–71; Thomas W. Lippman, *The Washington Post Deskbook on Style*, 2nd edition (New York: McGraw-Hill, 1989), 7.

5. Carl Bernstein and Bob Woodward, *All the President's Men* (New York: Simon & Schuster, 1974), 42–43.

6. To see some of the Internet resources described, go to http://people.yahoo.com; http://www.switchboard.com; and http://www.fec.gov/1996/sdrindex.htm.

7. Bruce William Oakley, "How Accurate Are Your Archives?" *Columbia Journalism Review* (March 13, 1998): 13.

8. Martin Fletcher, "Gingrich Wife Rules Out Bid for White House," *Times* (London), August 10, 1995; Margaret Carlson, "Newt's Bad Old Days," *Time* (August 21, 1995): 31.

9. Gail Sheehy, "The Inner Quest of Newt Gingrich," *Vanity Fair* (September 1995): at 220; "Newt Gingrich: Devalued Moral Values," *Flynt Report* 1, 40–41.

10. "The Mouse That Roars," *Newsweek* (September 20, 1999): 53.

11. Lanny J. Davis, *Truth to Tell: Tell It Early, Tell It All, Tell It Yourself: Notes from My White House Education* (New York: Free

Press, 1999); excerpted in "Scandal Management 101," *Washington Monthly* (May 1, 1999), 38.

12. Bryan Abas, "The Rumor About Romer," *Westword* (Denver), June 6–12, 1990, 10.

13. "Loose Lips," *Point* (Columbia, South Carolina), June 1996, quoted from an online archive (http://www.mindspring.com/~scpoint/point/9606/lips.html); Cindi Ross Scoppe, "Media Found No Facts in Beasley Rumors," *Columbia* (South Carolina) *State*, August 6, 1997, A9.

14. *Nuvo* article quoted by Jason Vest, "Secret Lives of Republicans, Part One," *Salon* (September 11, 1998): http://www.salonmagazine.com/news/1998/09/11newsb.html; John Strauss and Mary Beth Schneider, "Burton Says Magazine Is Looking for Dirt on Him," *Indianapolis Star*, September 1, 1998, A1; John Strauss and Mary Beth Schneider, "Burton Warns of 'Scandal Story,' " *Indianapolis News*, September 1, 1998, A1

15. Natalie Green, "What's Behind Paxon's Retreat," *Beat* (Buffalo, New York), March 6, 1998, e-mail copy sent to authors by the writer; Peter Perl, "Out of the House," *Washington Post Magazine* (April 12, 1998): 13; Sally Jacobs, "Home Rules," *Boston Globe*, November 3, 1998, E1; John McCaslin, "Inside the Beltway," *Washington Times*, January 7, 1999, A8.

16. John Yang, interview with authors, June 9, 1999.

17. We are not identifying the journalist out of deference to family members. Our conclusions on the rumors are based on personal interviews with reporters who covered the story, the journalist's friends, as well as some of those friends' printed accounts about the suicide.

18. Robert J. McCarthy, "Paxon Assails Airing of 'Rumors' Tied to Retirement," *Buffalo News*, March 10, 1998, 1B.

19. Green, "What's Behind Paxon's Retreat"; McCarthy, "Paxon Assails Airing of 'Rumors'."

20. Natalie Green, e-mail message to authors, September 20, 1999.

21. Paul M. Rodriguez, interview with authors, May 21, 1999.

22. Dennis Britton, interview with authors, June 14, 1999.

23. Florence Graves and Charles E. Shepard, "Packwood Accused of Sexual Advances," *Washington Post*, November 22, 1992, A1.

24. Josh Getlin, "Ring Around the Rumors," *Los Angeles Times*, March 5, 1997, E1; Jennet Conant, "Letter from New York:

The Ghost and Mr. Giuliani," *Vanity Fair*, September 1997, 154–164, 169–172.

25. Fred Kaplan, "Vanity Fair Out-Tabs the NY Tabs on Giuliani Story," *Boston Globe*, August 5, 1997, E1.

26. Adam Zagorin, "Catching the Starr Bug," *Time*, October 5, 1998, 33; Jeff Wilkinson, "Democrats' Lawyers Planned to Quiz Governor on Infidelity," *Columbia* (South Carolina) *State*, September 29, 1998, A1; "Beasley Again Denies Affair After Report," *The Herald* (Rock Hill, S.C.), September 29, 1998, 12A; Michael Sponhour, "'I've Been Faithful,' Governor Vows," *Columbia* (South Carolina) *State*, September 30, 1998, A1; Michael Sponhour, "Beasley Takes Offensive on Rumors," *The Post and Courier* (Charleston, S.C.), September 30, 1998, A1; "Letters," *Time*, November 22, 1998, 22.

27. Krista Reese, "The Lights Went Out in Georgia," *George* (May 1998): 70–73, 114–115; Kathey Pruitt, "Bowers Still Helping Her, Alleged Mistress Says," *Atlanta Journal and Constitution*, April 14, 1998, B3; Kathey Pruitt, "Bowers Says He Aided Ex-lover Out of Charity," *Atlanta Journal and Constitution*, April 15, 1998, E2; Kathey Pruitt, "Bowers Says He Stopped Payments to Ex-mistress," *Atlanta Journal and Constitution*, April 17, 1998, B3; Kathey Pruitt and Charmagne Helton, "Bowers' Ex-lover Talks to Local Media," *Atlanta Journal and Constitution*, April 30, 1998, D3.

28. James K. Glassman, "Matt Drudge, E-Journalist," *Washington Post*, June 9, 1998, A15.

CHAPTER 3

1. Larry King with Mark Stencel, *On the Line: The New Road to the White House* (New York: Harcourt Brace, 1993), 37.

2. "'Top Ten' by Gore," *Washington Post*, September 9, 1993, A19.

3. Pew Center for the People and the Press, "Fall Off Greater for Young Adults and Computer Users" (May 13, 1996): http://www.people-press.org/mediarpt.htm

4. Andy Soltis, "Love Gov Ditching Wife for His Ole Miss," *New York Post*, June 11, 1999, 14; Sue Anne Pressley, "Changing Partners in Dixie," *Washington Post*, July 13, 1999, C1; "Fordice Doesn't Regret Threats, Divorce, Pistol," *Jackson Clarion-Ledger*, August 7, 1999, 1A.

5. Bill Walsh, "Livingston Sex Life Won't Be Hustler Exposé: Larry Flynt Decides to Back Off after Listening to Personal Appeal from Congressman's Wife." *New Orleans Times-Picayune*, January 7, 1999, 6A; Joan McKinney, "Reports of Probe Ignored," *Baton Rouge Advocate*, December 22, 1998, 1A.

6. George Stuteville, John Strauss and Mary Beth Schneider, "A Telling Day: Burton Admits Affair," *Indianapolis Star*, September 5, 1998, A1; Alex Kuczynski, "Vanity Fair Won't Run Story on Representative," *New York Times*, October 12, 1998, 9; John Strauss, "Story Burton Saw Coming Is Published on Internet," *Indianapolis Star*, December 23, 1998, D1; Russ Baker, "Portrait of a Political 'Pit Bull,'" *Salon* (December 22, 1998): http://www.salon.com/news/1998/12/cov_22newsa.html; Juliet Eilperin and Howard Kurtz, "Burton Aide on Federal, Campaign Pay," *Washington Post*, December 23, 1998, A1.

CHAPTER 4

1. Peter J. Kent, "Bowers' Affair Not a Topic at GOP Breakfast," *Atlanta Journal and Constitution*, August 4, 1997, J2; Kathey Pruitt and Charles Walston, "GOP's Bowers Releases Personal Tax Returns," *Atlanta Journal and Constitution*, April 16, 1998, C8.

2. *Indianapolis Star*, September 29, 1998, B4; *Indianapolis Star*, October 6, 1998, D5; *Indianapolis Star*, October 13, 1998, B7; *Indianapolis Star*, October 21, 1998, B4.

3. Robert Timberg, *The Nightingale's Song* (New York: Touchstone, 1996), 239.

4. Timberg, *The Nightingale's Song*, 240.

5. *CNN Late Edition*, CNN, March 2, 1999; *Sunday Morning*, CBS, April 18, 1999; *60 Minutes*, CBS, June 6, 1999; *20/20*, ABC, September 8, 1999.

6. "Editorial: Why We Ran the Hyde Story," *Salon* (September 16, 1998): http://www.salonmagazine.com/news/1998/09/16newsc.html.

7. *Good Morning America*, ABC, September 17, 1998.

8. David Talbot, "'This Hypocrite Broke Up My Family,'" *Salon* (September 16, 1998): http://www.salonmagazine.com/news/1998/09/cov_16newsb.html.

9. Howard Kurtz, "Bureau Chief Ousted Over Hyde Affair Story," *Washington Post*, September 29, 1998, D1.

10. "Editorial: Why We Ran the Hyde Story," *Salon*; Howard Kurtz, "Hyde Story Stirs Hostilities," *Washington Post*, September 18, 1998, A1.

11. Larry J. Sabato, *Feeding Frenzy: How Attack Journalism Has Transformed American Politics* (New York: Free Press, 1991), 77–79, 97–98, 109–110.

12. *Today*, NBC, January 22, 1998.

13. *World News Tonight*, ABC, January 23, 1998.

14. John M. Broder, "Ex-intern Offered to Tell of Clinton Affair in Exchange for Immunity, Lawyers Report," *New York Times*, January 24, 1998 (from the newspaper's online archive).

15. *This Week*, ABC, January 25, 1998.

16. John F. Harris and Dan Balz, "Clinton More Forcefully Denies Having Had Affair or Urging Lies," *Washington Post*, January 27, 1998, A1.

17. Adam Cohen, "The Press and the Dress," *Time* (February 16, 1998): 52; Howard Kurtz, "With Leaks, Reporters Go with the Flow" *Washington Post*, February 9, 1998, B1.

18. "Lewinsky's Aug. 6 Grand Jury Testimony, Part 3," washingtonpost.com's "Clinton Accused" Special Report: http://www.washingtonpost.com/wp-srv/politics/special/clinton/stories/mltest080698_3.htm.

19. Bill Kovach and Tom Rosenstiel, *Warp Speed: America in the Age of Mixed Media* (New York: Century Foundation Press, 1999), 23, 139–143.

20. Michael Kinsley, "In Defense of Matt Drudge," *Time* (February 2, 1998): from the magazine's online archive, http://www.pathfinder.com/time/magazine/1998/dom/980202/kinsley.html.

21. *The Tonight Show*, NBC, March 31, 1999.

22. Maureen Dowd, "President Frat Boy?" *New York Times*, April 7, 1999 (from the newspaper's online archive); Maureen Dowd, "Puppy Love Politics," *New York Times*, June 9, 1999 (from the newspaper's online archive).

23. Steve Chapman, "The Real Problem With Bush's Past," *Chicago Tribune*, April 11, 1999, 19.

24. Ellen Joan Pollock, "Empty Chatter: Behind the Rumors About George Bush," *Wall Street Journal*, May 14, 1999, A1.

25. Helen Thorpe, "Go East, Young Man," *Texas Monthly*, June 1999 (from the magazine's online archive).

26. Lois Romano and George Lardner Jr., "1986: A Life-Changing Year," *Washington Post*, July 25, 1999, p. A1.

CHAPTER 5

1. NBC News Special Report, Burrelle's Information Services, November 8, 1995.

2. Dick Polman and Steve Goldstein, "Powell Looks More Like a Candidate," *Philadelphia Inquirer*, October 22, 1995, A1.

3. Howard Fineman, Eleanor Clift, and Evan Thomas, "Powell on the Brink," *Newsweek* (November 6, 1995): 36; Eleanor Clift and Evan Thomas with Tara Sonenshine, "Why the General's Wife Is a Reluctant Warrior," *Newsweek* (November 6, 1995): 39.

4. "Excerpts from Colin L. Powell's News Conference," *Washington Post*, November 9, 1995, A14.

5. Norman J. Ornstein, Thomas E. Mann, and Michael J. Malbin, *Vital Statistics on Congress, 1997–1998* (Washington, D.C.: Congressional Quarterly Inc., 1998), 61–62; "Departing the Hill," *CQ Weekly* (November 7, 1998): 2984.

6. Kathey Alexander, "Howard Bows Out, Citing Family Strain," *Atlanta Journal*, August 6, 1997, A1.

7. Jim Wooten, "Pierre Howard's Heart Wasn't on the Gubernatorial Campaign Trail," *Atlanta Journal and Constitution*, August 17, 1997, C5.

8. Pew Research Center for the People and the Press, "Striking the Balance: Audience Interests, Business Pressures and Journalists' Values" (March 30, 1999): http://www.people-press.org/press99rpt.htm.

9. Lisa de Moraes, "Monica Lewinsky Beats the Competition," *Washington Post*, March 5, 1999, C1.

10. Pew Research Center, "Striking the Balance."

11. Ken Olsen, "It's Williams Vs. Chenoweth, Part II," *Spokane Spokesman-Review*, October 18, 1998, A1; Ken Olsen, "Candidates Take Parting Shots," *Spokane Spokesman-Review*, October 30, 1998, A1.

12. Kathleen deLaski, e-mail message to authors, October 25, 1999.

CHAPTER 6

1. Kevin Merida, "Dole's 'Emergency' Divorce," *Washington Post*, August 7, 1996, A1.

2. Leonard Downie Jr., interview with authors, June 16, 1999.

3. Robert G. Kaiser, interview with authors, June 30, 1999; Blaine Harden, "A Seething Dole Intensifies Attack," *Washington Post*, October 26, 1996, A1.

4. Walter Isaacson, e-mail message to authors, November 5, 1999.

5. Howard Kurtz, "A Big Story—But Only Behind the Scenes," *Washington Post*, November 13, 1996, D1; Blaine Harden, "A Seething Dole Intensifies Attack," *Washington Post*, October 26, 1996, A1.

6. Leonard Downie Jr., interview with authors, November 9, 1999.

7. Harden, "A Seething Dole," A1.

8. Leonard Downie Jr., interview with authors, June 16, 1999.

9. Richard L. Berke, "McCain Having to Prove Himself Even in Arizona," *New York Times*, October 25, 1999, A1; "Arizona Paper Faults McCain on His Temper," *New York Times*, November 1, 1999, A15.

10. Larry J. Sabato, *Feeding Frenzy: How Attack Journalism Has Transformed American Politics* (New York: Free Press, 1991, 1993), 220–221, 270–271, 343.

11. Center for Media and Public Affairs, "Top Ten TV News Topics for 1998," *Media Monitor* 1 (January/February 1999): 1.

12. Robert G. Kaiser, interview with authors, June 30, 1999.

13. Dennis Britton, interview with authors, June 14, 1999.

14. Walter Isaacson, e-mail message to authors, November 5, 1999.

15. Larry J. Sabato and S. Robert Lichter, *When Should the Watchdogs Bark? Media Coverage of the Clinton Scandals* (Washington, D.C.: Center for Media and Public Affairs, 1994), 55–57.

16. Douglas Feiden, "Rudy Marriage on Rocks—Mag," *New York Daily News*, August 4, 1997, 5; Michele McPhee and Douglas Feiden, "Donna: It's a Family Affair," *New York Daily News*, August 5, 1997, 3.

17. David L. Lewis, "Vanity Fair Goofs on Itineraries," *New York Daily News*, August 5, 1997, 16; Keith J. Kelly, "Mag Sez Rudy Snitch Is a City Hall Insider," *New York Daily News*, August 8, 1997, 3.

18. Cindi Ross Scoppe, "Media Found No Facts in Beasley Rumors," *Columbia* (South Carolina) *State*, August 6, 1997, A9; Cindi Ross Scoppe, "A Summer Spent Investigating Intangible Allegations," *Columbia* (South Carolina) *State*, October 1, 1998, A16.

19. Scot Lehigh, "Of Alcohol, Politicians, and What Makes a News Story," *Boston Globe*, October 3, 1997, A15; Walter V. Robinson, "Flynn at the Vatican: His Mayoral Style Didn't Cut It," *Boston Globe*, October 3, 1997, A1.

20. Dan Popkey, Ken Miller, and Michelle Cole, "Chenoweth Regrets Relationship," *Idaho Statesman* (Boise), September 10, 1998, 1A.

21. Karen Baker, "Tough Decision Held Chenoweth Accountable for Her 'Integrity' Ad," *Idaho Statesman* (Boise), September 15, 1998, 6B.

22. Michele McLellan, "Ombudsmen Can Be Important Force, But Few Papers Have Them," *Portland Oregonian*, May 17, 1998, E6.

Index

About the Authors

Larry J. Sabato is director of the Center for Governmental Studies at the University of Virginia in Charlottesville and author of numerous books, including *Feeding Frenzy: How Attack Journalism Has Transformed American Politics.*

Mark Stencel is politics editor for washingtonpost.com and co-author with CNN's Larry King of *On the Line: The New Road to the White House.*

S. Robert Lichter is president of the Center for Media and Public Affairs in Washington, D.C., and editor of the online magazine *Newswatch.* His books include *The Media Elite* and *Good Intentions Make Bad News.*